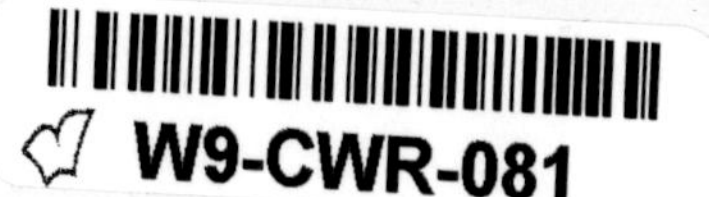
W9-CWR-081

# *The Diamond Anthology*

The Poetry Society of America
Founded 1910

# THE DIAMOND ANTHOLOGY

Edited by Charles Angoff, Gustav Davidson, Hyacinthe Hill, and A. M. Sullivan

*Foreword by Charles Angoff*



South Brunswick and New York
A. S. Barnes and Company
*for the*
Poetry Society of America

Library of Congress Catalogue Card Number: 78-155795

A. S. Barnes and Co., Inc.
Cranbury, New Jersey 08512

ISBN 0-498-07950-3

Printed in the United States of America

*In Memory of*
*Gustav Davidson*
*(1895–1971)*

# Contents

# *Foreword*

This, the third anthology of poems by members of The Poetry Society of America—the first appeared in 1946 and the second in 1960—has significance beyond the pleasure and delight to be derived from reading its contents. It celebrates two events: the sixtieth anniversary of the Society and the Society's return to where it came into being in 1910, the historic National Arts Club in Gramercy Park.

It is good to be back home, and the age of sixty, to a poetry society as to an individual poet, is an exhilarating event. It is a moment of pause for further and deeper joys, for more comforting reflections, for greater and more encompassing loves. Ralph Waldo Emerson said the proper words:

Spring still makes Spring in the mind
When sixty years are told:
Love wakes anew this throbbing heart
And we are never old.

A glance at the list of founders, officers, and other members of the Society in the six decades of its existence indicates the motives behind its establishment, the quality of its deliberations, and the extent of its influence. A few of the eminent names follow: Witter Bynner, John Erskine, Arthur Guiterman, Leonora Speyer, Alfred Kreymborg, Robert Hillyer, Bliss Carman, Julian Hawthorne, Richard Le Gallienne, Percy MacKaye, Edwin

Markham, Joaquin Miller, Lizette Woodworth Reese, George Santayana, George Sterling, Ridgely Torrence, Robert Frost, Ludwig Lewisohn, Theodore Dreiser, Stephen Vincent Benet, George E. Woodberry, William Rose Benet, Willa Cather, Robert P. T. Coffin, George Dillon, Arthur Davison Ficke, John Gould Fletcher, Oliver St. John Gogarty, Du Bose Heyward, Robinson Jeffers, Joyce Kilmer, Christopher La Farge, Vachel Lindsay, Amy Lowell, John Masefield, Edgar Lee Masters, David Morton, Alfred Noyes, Edwin Arlington Robinson, Carl Sandburg, Alan Seeger, Wallace Stevens, Sara Teasdale, Elinor Wylie.

This listing is confined to the poets who have joined

> The innumerable caravan, which moves
> To that mysterious realm, where each shall take
> His chamber in the silent halls of death . . .

A long and glorious roster that makes it unnecessary to "confirm with facts" the purposes of the Society as stated in Article III of the Constitution: "to secure wider recognition for poetry as one of the important forces making for a higher cultural life: to kindle a more intelligent appreciation of poetry: and to do such other acts as may be deemed appropriate to assist poets, especially younger American poets."

The membership of the Society is selective, and hence small, in the neighborhood of 700. It conducts a Poetry Workshop for beginning and experienced poets. It holds public monthly meetings devoted to the critical discussion of poems anonymously submitted by members, and to the presentation of talks about every major aspect of poetry as an art and as an exploration of philosophies of life; it publishes centenary-memoir-anthologies of former members; and it attempts to expand the market for the publication of poetry and for the purchase of magazines and books of poetry. The Poetry Society of America takes chief credit for the establishment of the Pulitzer Award for Poetry, and virtually everyone who has won the Award has been a member of the Society.

The quality of the poetry produced by members of the Society is fully attested by this third anthology. A board of four was appointed by the President to select one poem, if deemed worthy, from three submitted by every member. There were no conditions whatsoever as to type, form, or attitude. The only criterion was: is it good poetry? Happily, there was an avalanche of poems to choose from. The editors believe that the present anthology, besides its sheer poetical value, will also have importance in the literary annals of the United States.

A special word of thanks to Gustav Davidson, Hyacinthe Hill, and A. M. Sullivan, associated with me in preparing the anthology; also to Madeline Mason and Louise Townsend Nicholl for their labors in getting the biographical notes into shape.

Charles Angoff
President,
The Poetry Society
of America

# *The Diamond Anthology*

## *George Abbe*

### THE CATERPILLAR

I lay upon the soft of day,
the green of bounty shyly known.
The light came through my windows free,
the branches of my trust were plain,
fretting a bronzed and cordial sky.

All, all about me, people went
at duties that would make me safe;
their strength was my astonishment;
and, godly, they knew no mistake.

But all at once, the couch, the room
broke outward to the sweltering lawn;
the floors for treasured footsteps waned,
the walls whose bright designs were drawn
by innocence, sank without sound.

I placed my hand on the lush grass:
under it, suffocating calm
beat like the shadow of a wound;
the heat, upwavering to my bone,
fused me to coil of ugliness.

And there, in a fold of the lawn's flesh,
scar from a careless human heel,
a caterpillar, hued intense,
unwound from earth, uprose immense,
loomed over me and numbed my gaze.

And now, the sun dimmed; high and thick
from hill to hill, from house to house,
a bagworm tent strung huge and coarse;
within its gray the worms writhed black;
flickered its surface with coiling young;
heavy as breast it strove to break;
the air grew vile; the sun was gone.

## *Ellen Acton*

### FRENCH BARGES

Through France the long black barges glide,
Laden with wood or coal or stone,
Or heaped with lustrous fruit, they slide
Beneath the bridges of the Seine,
The swift Garonne, the endless Loire,
Manned by shrewd, complacent men
Who smoke, or fish, or whittle dreams,
Or on old towpaths manage teams.

A barge wife, dark against the sun,
Dries children's clothes beside the hatch.
Incurious, she waves to none.
Along the banks, the fishermen
Look up, take cognizance, and then,
Immobile, tend their lines again.
The long black stack, aslant the sky,
Sends up a whorl of yellow smoke.
The barge toots by.

## *Marjorie Louise Agnew*

### LINES UPON LEAVING A DWELLING

I will look in the mirror this one last time
And leave my face in the glass
To disturb those who come after me.
It will float on the still silver lake,
Eyes closed, like a shut water lily.
Let them wonder what I was like,
At the tiny hoof-prints in the garden,
The strange red stone facing East,
As the rush of cold wind down the stair,
As they mount, hand in hand, where we were. . . .

## *Conrad Aiken*

### THE CRYSTAL

What time is it now, brother Pythagoras, by the pale stone
set like a jewel in the brow of Sheepfold Hill?
There where the little spider, your geometrist,
shrinks from autumn in the curl of a leaf,
his torn world blown in the wind? What time, tonight,
under the motionless mill-wheel, in the pouring brook,
which bears to the sea—O *thalassa, thalassa,*
*pasa thalassa,* for the sea is still the sea—
the flickering fins, unnumbered, which will return thence
in April or May? By the dial in Samos what hour?
Or in Babylon among the Magi?

Your forefoot ploughs
over the floating Pole Star, Ionian foam
wets once again the gemmed sandal, as westward still
the oars beat time, and the sail runs out, in the wake
of Samian Kolaios.

Not you for bars of silver,
nor to trade wool or wine or raisins for tin,
and not to return to Samos, nor with regret, but rather—
listen!—as with these migrants who now above us
whirl the night air with clamor of wings and voices,
southward voyaging, the caucus of robins,
choosing, like you, a propitious hour.

So the page turns
always in the middle of a sentence, the beginning of a
meaning;
the poem breaks in two. So the prayer, the invocation,
and the revelation, are suspended in our lives,
suspended in a thought. Just as now,
still there in the dark at the prow of your galley,
your hand on the cleat, you observe the division of water,
the division of phosphor, yourself the divider,
and the law in the wave, and the law in the eye;
observing, too, with delight; and remembering
how once on the headland of Bathy at daybreak
you sacrificed a hundred oxen to your godfather, Apollo,
or was it forty or fifty,
and the occasion for it: your vision
of the triangle's godgiven secret, the song of the square
echoing the squares.

Long ago: far away:
wave-length and trough-length: the little Pan's Pipe
plaintive and sweet on the water at midnight:
yet audible still to the infinitesimal
tambourine of the eardrum. And now you are sixty,
the beard is of sea-moss. At Delphi
you set foot on the salt shingle, climbed

up the path through the rocks to the temple,
where priestesses dreamed with their oakleaves.
What warning or promise from the *tripous?* What cryptic
oracle flung from the sun on the mountain
to bear on the sea-track that beats to the west?
Daybreak it was, with long shadows. Far down,
at the foot of the gorge, you could measure
the toy groves of olives, the hearse-plumes of cypress,
and daisies danced in a ring, and the poppies
in the grass and wild thyme around you
went running, and crackling like fire. Alas!
a few columns, only, still stand there,
and the wild fig roots in the wall. And now,
your galleys hush west on the sea,
as you, old migrant, set sail once again
(like those fins down the stairs to the bay)
with your wife and your sons, and the grandchildren
swaddled,
your gear and your goats and your handmaids;
setting forth as aforetime to Thebes.
While we,
secret and silent, sealed off in the west,
sit still and await you. In a different world,
and yet foreseen in your crystal:
the numbers known to your golden abacus,
and the strings that corded your lyre.

II

Six o'clock, here, in the western world, a west
unknown to sailor Kolaios, or the porters of Tartessus.
Stony Brook ferries its fins to the sea. Four bells
sing now in the fisherman's lighted cabin
above the brass binnacle and the floating compass.
Six o'clock in the cone of the Equinox, the bells
echo over mud-flats, sift through the nets

where mackerel flap and flash in the pools,
and over the oyster-beds, the shells of the razor-fish,
borne inland, to be echoed again
by the austere bell in the puritan steeple.
At seven, in the ancient farmhouse,
cocktails sparkle on the tray, the careful answer
succeeds the casual question, a reasoned dishevelment
ruffling quietly the day's or the hour's issue.
Our names, those we were born with,
or those we were not born with, since all are born
nameless,
become the material, or the figment, if we wish,
of which to weave, and then unweave, ourselves.
Our lives, those we inherited, of which
none can claim ownership in fee simple, but only
a tenant's lease, of unpredictable duration,
rented houses from which have already departed perhaps
those others, our other selves, the children:
ourselves in these on our way beyond death
to become the undying succession of inheritors:
these and other aspects of the immortal moment
glow into consciousness for laughter or tears,
an instant of sympathy or misunderstanding, an exchange
of human touch or tact, or agreement, soon silent.
And here, as in the silence, too, that follows,
like the peacock's eye of shadow round the lifted candle,
is the tacit acceptance of death. We invoke,
and what is life but an invocation,
the shore beyond the vortex, the light beyond the dark,
the number beneath the name. We shall not be here
to pour the bright cocktails, while we listen
to the throb of migrant wings in the night air,
the chorus of departing voices, the bells from the bay;
and yet, brother Pythagoras, like you,
who still set your sail this night to the west,

we too shall be held so. After our deaths
we too shall be held so. And thus, brought together.

III

And yet, if this were so, but in another sense:
the immortality, perhaps, of a different sort:
or death somehow of a different kind: and if it were true,
as in the myth of All Hallows at this season,
when frost beards the pumpkin, and the last apple
thuds to bare earth; and if, from our graves,
whether at Metapontum by the fields of corn,
or by the muddy river at Isle of Hope,
or under the Acropolis on the hill of rocks,
with the moon's shield brazen above us: yes, if, called
by name,
you there, I here, we could arise,
and make our way in the dark to the road's edge
for a day or a night of the familiar habits;
what time would it be, brother Pythagoras,
for what custom, and what place?
All life
is ritual, or becomes so: the elusive pattern
unfolds its arcanum of observances,
measured in time, and measured by time, as the heartbeat
measures the blood. Each action, no matter how simple,
is precious in itself, as part of the devotion,
our devotion to life. And what part of this ritual
would we choose for reenactment? What rite
single out to return for? After the long silence,
and the long sleep, wherein has been never
configuration of dream; no light, no shape;
not the geometer's triangle, flashing in sun,
to be resolved in reason, no, nor the poet's mirage of
landscape,

brilliant as the image in the finder of a camera,
nor the gem-carver's little emerald, with lyre and cupido,
or the sculptor's bronze, the *cire-perdue,*
an art fetched from Egypt: no, no sound, no color:
what then would we choose? Carver of gems, lover of
crystal,
savior-god of Croton! can you yet soothsay?

Easy enough, it would be, to find in the darkness
the familiar roadside, the shape of a known tree,
and then, how naturally, alas, the faded signpost
stuck in the sand: and on it to make out with joy
the names that point homeward. And easy enough
to fly then as the bee flies, to home as to hive.
And arrived there, to find the door open,
the fire on the hearth, the pot on the trivet,
the dish on the table—with a red rim—for grapes,
and the ripe blue cluster; to feel with one's foot
the slope of the floorboard, and on it the scars
ridged by the adze; the shelves bright with bowls,
and the floor bright with mats, and the walls
bright with pictures. And then, to lift gently
the one thing most loved: as if in this thing
one could best hold them all. And thus, it might be
a spoon from one's childhood: a shell of thin silver,
a handle shaped like a tiny brick chimney,
atop of it, perching, a dwarf with a horn,
a curled horn tilted to heaven.
In this,
to achieve the resumption, the chained implication,
backward, then forward, of the whole of one's life.

Too simple perhaps? Or an example, only.
For, to which house, of the many houses,
and all of them loved, would one fare first?

To which altar of the many altars, the changing
gods, with their changing attributes? Which city
of the many dear cities? Samos, with its wall,
and the port, and the Hera Temple, and the tunnel
carved through the rock by Eupalinos, to bring water
for the three brave fountains, praised by Herodotus?
Or Croton, of the Brotherhood? Who can say?
Perhaps for none of these, but, more simply,
for the pronunciation, softly, of a single name:
the observation, precisely, of a single flower:
white crocus, white hyacinth. Or perhaps
we would return if only once more to remember
something secret and precious, but forgotten: something
intended,
but never performed: begun, but not finished.
Or else, to notice, but now with a more careful love,
the little hooked claws, bent down, of the clover:
the white geometry, in clearest numbers,
of those little asters, or asterisks, the snow.
Samples, examples!
And perhaps too concrete. The heart might so choose,
but what of the mind? All very well
the sight or the sound, the taste or the feeling, the touch
or the texture. And, as in a dream,
To combine them—delicious! Thus, a ring of your father's,
Mnesarchos, the gem-carver: you watch him at work,
yourself still a boy, and both silent:
the emerald held in a vice, then the green
ice of the clear stone gives up its goddess,
the tiny wave bears up its Venus, green foam
on the brow and the shoulder. The image?
Of course! But beneath or behind it
the knowledge, the craft: and the art, above all.
Would it not be for this, for ruler and compass,
brother Pythagoras, that we would return?

For both: the one is the other. In each lies the other.
Design shines implicit in the blind moment
of self-forgetful perception: belief is steadfast
in the putting forth of a hand, as in the first
wingbeat, or extension of a claw; the law
unfolding and infolding forever.
It would be for this
Apollonian fountain of the forever unfolding,
the forever-together, ourselves but a leaf
on the fountain of tree, that we would return:
the crystal self-shaping, the godhead designing the god.
For this moment of vision, we would return.

### IV

The admirations come early, crowd through
the lenses of light and the lenses of the eye,
such sudden and inimitable shapes, such colors
confusing and confused, the vast but orderly
outpouring and downpouring and inpouring—who but
a god could distribute so many and so various,
but what god and where? Not Aladdin
in the dark cave walking on jewels and precious stones,
on diamonds and rubies, brushing the walls
of topaz and opal, ever went among such wonders
or was ever so dazzled. The wind's serpent
sibilant and silver in a field of barley
insinuates a pattern, the concentric
ripples in a fountain perpetuate another
the quartz crystal offers a pyramid, and two together,
joined, a cube! Where burns not or shines not
purity of line? The veins of the myrtle
are alive with it, the carpenter's board
diagrams it in a cross-section of history, life
empanelled golden in a design. What does not your hand
turn up or over, living or inanimate,

large or small, that does not signal
the miracle of interconnectedness
the beams meeting and crossing in the eye and the mind
as also in the sun? How can you set end to it
where is no ending and no beginning
save in the one that becomes the many, the many
that compose the one? How shall we praise the forms?
Algebra shines, the rose-tree perfects with precision
its love the rose, the rose perfects with precision
its love the seed, the seed perfects with precision
its love the tree. How shall we praise the numbers?
Geometry measures an arc of orchard an arc of sky
the inward march and arch of the mind. Things
are numbers. Numbers are the shape
given to things, immanent in things past and present
as in the things to come. Not water nor fire
nor Anaximander's cloud nor only
the inexhaustible and unknowable flux which Heraclitus
in vain exhorted to be still, but number
that buds and breaks from number, unfolds in number,
blossoms in number, is born and dies in number.

And the sounds too, your loves the sounds:
In these to find the final of harmonies, the seven
unequal strings of the lyre, the seven notes to be
intertwined or countered, doubled or trebled or wreathed;
seven strings for the seven sages, to each
the *tripous* awarded, as to Pherekydes your teacher:
but not to yourself, except in
the little tripod of silver you minted
for the coins of Croton. And then, ringing all,
encircling the worlds and the god's central fire,
the revolving spheres and the music they chorus
too perfect for hearing.
The admirations
come early, stay long, multiply marvelously,

as if of their own volition. In such confusion
what answer for order? The odd and the even,
the prime and the solid, the plane and the oblong:
numbers, shapes, sounds, measurements, all these
to be studied and observed with joy, with passion,
the wind's serpent to be followed where it
vanishes in a spiral of silver through the wheatfield
the ripples to be pursued as they ply outward
over the fountain-face of cloud-flattering water
plangency and pitch of the lyre's note
to be judged exactly by the length of the tight string
notched in the edge of the tortoise-shell:
crystal and asphodel and snowflake
alike melting in the palm of the mind, and the mind
admiring its own admirations, in these too
uncovering the miracle of number: all, at last,
transparent, inward and outward, the one
everlasting of experience, a pure delight.

V

What is the voyage and who is the voyager?
Who is it now hoisting the sail
casting off the rope and running out the oars
the helmsman with his hand on the tiller
and his eyes turned to windward? What time is it now
in the westward pour of the worlds and the westward
pour of the mind? Like a centipede on a mirror
the galley stands still in a blaze of light
and yet swims forward: on the mirror of eternity
glitters like a golden scarab: and the ranked oars
strike down in harmony beat down in unison
churn up the water to phosphor and foam
and yet like the galley are still.
So you

still stand there, your hand on the tiller,
at the center of your thought, which is timeless,
yourself become crystal. While we,
still locked in the west, yet are present before you,
and wait and are silent.
                                        In the ancient farmhouse
which has now become your temple
we listen again to the caucus of robins
the whistle of migrant voices and wings
the turn of the great glass of season.
You taught the migration of souls: all things
must continue, since numbers are deathless:
the mind, like these migrants, crosses all seasons,
and thought, like these cries, is immortal.
The cocktails sparkle, are an oblation.
We pour for the gods, and will always,
you there, we here, and the others who follow,
pour thus in communion. Separate in time,
and yet not separate. Making oblation
in a single moment of consciousness
to the endless forever-together.
                                                  This night
we all set sail for the west.

## *Margaret Albanese*

### INTERPRETER AT TRIAL

Here in the courtroom
time has flattened itself against the wall.
The prisoner, thrust from the crooked doorway,

stands where three o'clock hangs from a black hook,
the mind stops short of the word,
and the gathered evidence of terror burns at hand.

Here I confront accuser and accused,
and negative as the air that moves between,
keep myself from cause and consequence,
with what I say tempered
to the slain flock and the wolf feeding.
Yet past and present fuse in an old error
and resolution fails, and I remember
that through the hazards of the crooked year
however the mind may bear its cold,
his day begins and ends with a tin tray.

## *Daisy Aldan*

### I AWAKE IN THESE HILLS

I awake into the breathing breast of memory
where I flow, mercury blue: the eloquent
arrested streams mineralizing
engraved in the crags: you mineralizing
scars into my becoming. After the faltering

earthquake, trying to re-arrange tranquility
into the footsteps of presence: this quicksilver,
thunder, altering to granite:
Yesterday, lightning in the fragrance of linden
too quick for focus: Your voice—"Kein Abschiedskummer!"

I was dying into your receding on the path
of dark spruce and roses: you revolving among

the train wheels: Echo of a wail across
the puzzling continent of you. Here, the wound
of your face wavering on the rocks.

## *Frances Alexander*

### CONVERSATION WITH A LAMB

There was so much I could not tell him,
That little white lamb who queried me.
I could not answer his inquisitive bleating
I was as much in question as he.

"The world is round, that much we have proven;
And many night stars are as large as the sun;
And all that you see on this leafy hillside
Was arranged in love by a Greater One.

"You are His symbol in holy scriptures
The wolf shall dwell with the lamb in peace
The little hills leap like lambs in gladness
The unblemished Lamb bring sin's release.

"Gentleness blends in your form and your crying
Sorrow and sacrifice echo your name;
Love and the Lamb hold out against hating
That's why you're here, that's why you came."

When I had finished my inadequate answer,
I but a strange tall creature to him,
He queried again in gentle rebuttal
Ba-ahed and demurred, then rejoined his peers

Leaving me lessoned with laughter and wonder
At his neat fitting flannels and his little pink ears.

## *Sara Van Alstyne Allen*

### BEACH CAROUSEL IN WINTER

The splendid horses are ready to run forever,
But summer is over.
They stand deserted under the canvas cover,
Silver and tarnished gold, and black, and dappled grey,
Their manes blown wide in the wind of a warmer day.
Their heads are proud as they rear and leap in their places.
Their eyes are bright; the dream of speed in their faces.

The bitter wind billows the canvas cover.
The carousel shudders as though at the touch of a lover,
Remembering the laughter of children,
The music strident and thin,
And the round, the magical ring of golden tin,
Forever eluding the young, uplifted hands.
Summer is over. The music is gone.
The wind outside blows the brittle snow
Over the winter sands.

## *Julia Cooley Altrocchi*

### BEGGAR OF EGYPT

Asleep in the red dust
Of Thebes the beggar lies,

Wrapped in his nullity,
Crowned with jewel-head flies.

In flood where no heart breaks
Let him drown fact awhile,
On gold-felucca streams,
Lord of the inner Nile.

Grant him, in sackcloth sleep,
The gift of what he seems,
Prince of the Triple Crown,
Heir of dynastic dreams.

He knows the greater self
Oblivion may bring.
Though beggar when he wakes,
Asleep he is god-king.

## *Dorothy Alyea*

### PICTURE SHOW

Faded women, like dull embers
Sit in the darkened house of shadows
Watching the ghosts on the screen dancing,
Mourning their loss of the bright meadows.

Where are their men? The Sons of Morning
Who taught the lust that the screen remembers,
Who left the weight of their kisses burning
On lips lifted to light romancing
From the leaves' fall to the leaves' turning
Over and over to new Septembers.

Pale the girl from the virgin bed.
Paler the dead.

Where are the men the war has taken
Out of the streets of light shining
Down through the rain on the women walking?
Gone into nightmares of rain streaming
Into crevasses by guns shaken,
To make a bed in the shell's crater.

Where is the boy of the loud talking
With whistle and jeer for the screen satyr
And a hand on the breast of the girl dreaming,
Left to a bed he has never taken.

The screen fades, the music's on.
The show is done.

## *Bernice Ames*

### THE GATHERING

From river ledges and the fire under alders
I gather them slowly on long stems
these friends who nod in my direction
seeing in me as in a mirror
some inner reaching, some feature their own.

And when we are easy, petal to petal
they push me into myself.
Under their blaze of approval, or disdain
I rise and color, pulled
out of the darkness of my own intent.

Composed, I can give to them—
fragrance to one, pale shadows another
until I am parched and leafless.
Then I lean over their flowering
to gather myself again.

## *Evelyn Ames*

### THE WHIPPET

So delicate he looked, so royal,
He made quite plausible those tales
Of princes transformed by a spell.
Leashed to a royal hand, his forebears
Stand proudly in tapestries' *mille fleurs.*

Few whites were whiter—swans, perhaps,
And white quartz pebbles, certain shells.
In sun, the white was tinctured pink;
In shade, leaned—as clouds do—to blue.
Running, he made bird-flying look slow.

Couchant, with his front paws crossed,
He'd outstare you, eyes down to slits,
The dignity of cats mixed with
Dog love. How he fought to make barks talk,
And trembled, trying not to obtrude!

On the last afternoon, I saw
All of his selfhood draw at once
To one fine, still point; under a birch
(His sister tree) his white grace pled,
See what I am! Look at me well!

And even as we faced each other,
The convergence was being set:
Home-hurrying car and roadside rabbit,
Dog bred to give a rabbit chase.
Each took his cue, two made it—safe.

Our connection snapped. The caved-in shell
That shuddered its life out in my lap
Was so absorbed in dying—or was it
Resisting death?—I had to shout
Across the gap, "*You* are all right!"

For so it seemed. Some presence there
Inside that torn-up coat maintained
An air of great, impersonal calm.
But who that was I could not name,
For all the eight years we had shared.

## *Forrest Anderson*

### FOG

A murk covers all and all is changed
The known turns unfamiliar. Each next step you take is
over the brink, to risk collision, in this impalpable element
with some Menace looming up, but

he turns out to be merely pitiable: another
like you who like to prowl through this mysterious
pall, meet perhaps Adventure, or for a dead dream
finally to weep. Time is turned

liquid now. You can hear it drip, drop,

fall away (discreet as irrevocable things are) so quiet
shroud and bier, under a gloriously tender light
shattered by the wails of sirens down the line:

Wild spirits—ships—crying out in a despair of loneliness
and your eyes burn to make out the shape
approaching. is it that of The Lost Continent of Love
whose coasts you would explore in every way?

Then you come face to face
          suddenly with the Stranger
          to find he is
                    only yourself again.

## *John Williams Andrews*

### WALL BUILDERS

Wall-builders:
Stone bolts in mowings,
Great hands under the boulders,
Wall-stones lifted and wedged,
Walls built and soils released
For crops' fruitfulness.

Those were times of skies parochial,
Roots beneath elm trees, under the white spires,
Centered, but in illusion reaching out
To draw horizons and harp-bearing clouds;
When, in the midnight mind,
Sometimes, flashes of star-fire raged;
When ladders dropped from heaven
Shook off the lethal legacies of earth

To strike for far-off portals;
Times when, O watchers,
It was not trees that let the ladders down,
Nor chattering voices yet the ancestry.

Dreams then were palpable, and ghosts
Went literal haunting, and second sight
Rode in veiled splendor on the inbred hills.
Man, in the Image,
Walked a rebellious earth,
Self not yet divisible, not yet
The unripe culture of the clear,
No witchcraft of the horizontal
To shift and bound the contours of the soul.

O we are wise!
O we are the tall towers!
Proudly we crampon to the highest hills,
Corking the canyons,
Pushing the marshes
Against the waders and the trumpeters,
High space our habitat,
The moon stripped of its wonder,
Death reparcelled in bitter packages
Because we move with egos in our eyes.

O I am great!
I, builder,
I, mountain-mover,
I, sea-penetrator,
I, child of the Cosmos!

Down my nose
I stare at the wall-builders.
They could not step from continent to continent,
Pinning the ears of Atlantic to Pacific.

They could not menace the moon.
They could not go abroad in a blast-off with computers
To give them the proper turn-off for Venus,
Avoiding the singed backsides
At the second star to the right before the sun!

I have abolished all things but me.
I have built my own walls: they stand on the edge of a
button.
I worship them,
Raising my hands in panic as they teeter.

## *Charles Angoff*

### SONG FOR THE EVE OF THE SABBATH

Time is the
Echo of
Elohim.

This evening
Is the holy
Silence of
Eternity.

Good and
Evil embrace
And vanish
In the bosom
Of the Sabbath.

The hour of
Regret has

Come, and
Tomorrow
Can be heard
The whisper of
Infinity.

Be still.
All being is
Listening

The bride of
Time is
Singing.

## *Philip Appleman*

### MEMO TO THE 21st CENTURY

It was like this once: sprinklers mixed
our marigolds with someone else's
phlox, and the sidewalks under maple trees
were lacy with August shade,
and the whistles called at eight and fathers walked
to work, and when they blew again,
men in tired blue shirts followed
their shadows home to grass.
That is how it was
in Indiana.

Towns fingered out to country once,
where brown-eyed daisies waved a fringe on orchards
and cattle munched at clover, and
fishermen sat in rowboats and were silent,

and on gravel roads, boys and girls
stopped their cars and felt the moon and touched,
and the quiet moments ringed and focussed
lakes    moon    flowers.
That is how it was
in Indiana.

But we are moving out, now,
scraping the world smooth where apples blossomed,
paving it over for cars. In the spring,
before the clover goes purple,
we mean to scrape the hayfield, and
next year the hickory woods:
we are pushing on, our giant scrapers snarling—
and I think of you, the billions of you, wrapped
in your twenty-first-century concrete,
and I want to call to you, to let you know
that if you dig down, claw your way
down past wires and pipes
and sewers and subways, you will find
a crumbly stuff called
earth. Listen:
in Indiana once, things
grew in it.

## *Sarah Leeds Ash*

### DUSK WATER

In that deep hour when the sea of dusk—
dusk water—trails dark fingers down the shore,
touches the wind with evanescent musk,
discards the afternoon, then from the door

of evening come intemperate silences,
louder than night-sound, louder than the sea,
whose minor music holds and balances
refluent sorrows on the wave of day.

So flows the sea of dusk across the mind
in that deep hour when discordant light
ebbs with the afternoon. The heart resigned
to softer footfall of persuasive night
recalls old sorrow and is taciturn;
now grief is only wind in marsh and fern.

## *Helen P. Avery*

### THE VENUS OF RHODES

Waves for centuries
Caressed her hair,
Explored her marble knees,
Smoothed with watery hands
Her thighs and breasts
Till curves grew muted.
Her nearly melted face
Breathes less
Of the cold sea floor
Than of Love's embrace.

## *Mary Newton Baldwin*

### ON PLANTING A YOUNG MAPLE

This tree I plant will never grow
As high as joy, as wide as woe;
But it will grow as maples do
Tall and broad and good to view.

It will not get its growth as soon
As boys who change from moon to moon;
But with its sweetness it will bring
Joy to children in the spring.

It is too young to shelter me
In years of my infirmity,
But in its shade young love will lie
And old men pause when passing by.

## *Eva Bán*

### BIAFRA CHILDREN

The children full of light
step slowly, the sun streams
down

in perfect red. Their eyes
are widely open
tears are dried—
they move their hands a little.

Sun is all around them
like a sea forever circling;
the jungle broods in age-old
exploding leafy strength
as one by one the children die
gnawing a root or simply
                                        standing there
looking at us with pity and
                                        contempt.

## *Melanie Gordon Barber*

### MIRABILE DICTU

My fingers touch upon my wrist—
The reassuring sign appears
As it has done these fifty years.
Each mystic moment I am blest
With summer singing in my breast.
As Moses heard it from the bush,
And Helen Keller in midnight hush,
I *feel* The Word made manifest.

One with that myriad joyous choir,
Along with lyre-bird, lark and Dove,
I hymn the Truth revealed to me
Through this immediate semaphore.
Something He tells me of His love,
Whispering in my scarlet tree.

## *Willis Barnstone*

### PATMOS

The dream ends here. Beyond these solitary whales
    and seven stars
we wake. Here is peace. It is not ours.
By steamer we came to the cave of the revelation
    where a boy is blowing bubblegum
    in the yellow air by the candles.
Is this the end? We lose and we begin, and climb
    nervously. Wind is wild noise.
Sun bakes the white crenelation on the hilltop
    monastery
The heavens open and a white horse steps
    on mountains in the water.
Can we see? The daystars fall like figs
    cast down by the windmill gale.
The sea is glass mingled with fire.
Fire in us who love. We lose. We wake.
    On the wharf an octopus, in
    each tentacle a horse of salt
    shining like the seven stars.
The dream ends here. Fire in us who lose.
    In the dark cave we see.

## *Isabel Harriss Barr*

### MADAKET BEACH

They speak of time, as if the hour were split
Into atomic parts, each grooved to each,

And barbed with sixty seconds; the knife-whet
Enmeshed, to chill with its steel touch

Both you and me. It is not true. There on the broad,
Cleft beach at Madaket, pillowed on sand
You asked, "Where has the morning gone?" The tide,
A net of shells, moved closer to my hand.

And then the sea came in and flooding, swept
In one momentous wave, toward the green dune.
The spindly sandpiper stopped short and leapt
To air, while time rose, circled and was gone.

## *Marguerite Enlow Barze*

### I CHOOSE IT OVER HELL

Never having been one who could
Start-his-mouth-going-and-go-off-and-leave-it-going
I must stay with my mouthful of words—taste,
Swallow down, assimilate meanings,
By writing them in before letting them out.
Is it a game I play slyly to
Outwit head-ache, stomach-ache, heart-ache?

Born to love words as my mother loved flowers,
My doctor father a stethoscope,
I seed-bed and water them, peer and listen
For nuance of growth, color of symptom, till
Buds evolve into phrases that fruit
To ripeness to pop in my mouth.

Yet I am no Lord-of-the-word,

A tongue-tart master who makes them spring up,
Wither or die, stay green, turn purple;
Rather, words intwist me, branch to root,
In private consumption for public confession
And such occlusion brings freedom. If
A game, slyly or not, I play it for keeps.

## *Madeline Bass*

### FATHER
son

David mourned
funny
not for the loss of what he had
had
but for the finality
of never having
had
something
that might have been
now lost
forever.
David clung
to a raggy image
of what was not
warm flesh but
gave his
and bent lower
to find the fat
of his own belly
the warm flow
of his own fathering

to hear that
elegy
suddenly echoed
that his own son
would sooner or later
sing.

## *Laura Benét*

### ONE WOMAN

She was a greening tree that sent forth shoots,
Courting life through warm and wintry days.
There came a bitter storm that shook her roots—
She never turned her face again toward praise,
Met eyes of men, touched childhood's tender fingers;
Bending in her despair became a shell.
Her leaves dropped soon, her blossoms did not linger,
Aloof, alone, she kept her citadel.
So passed her prime. The end of life drew on,
Sun, shade and resignation did the rest.
Slowly she took on beauty, grew serene,
While clasping ancient sorrow to her breast.
As countless trees reach skyward ere they go,
So was her image. Late spring in the snow.

# *Gertrude Ryder Bennett*

## THE HARVESTERS

Here someone made an effort to outwit
  The weather and the years. The beams were hewn
By hand and pegged together. Trees were split
  For massive shingles and by harvest moon
This farmhouse challenged all the years ahead.
  This was expression of the permanent.
But now the owner of the farm is dead
  And all the demons of the storm have spent
Their strength and crushed it in a ruined heap.
  But where the garden stood the golden glow
Raises its little suns. The roses creep
  Over decay and still the lilacs grow.
Each spring frail roots renew themselves in birth
To seek their heritage, these meek of earth.

They call this farm abandoned yet each year
  There is a host of those who garner crops.
With grave authority they gather here.
  They are the harvesters and nothing stops
Their fierce incessant labor. Porcupines
  Scale the old boughs of knotted apple trees
To taste the summer. Underneath the vines
  Long since unpruned, the deer stamp in the breeze.
And browse where once the kitchen garden grew.
  The chipmunks make a business taking seeds.
The squirrels reap. The trellis, all askew,
  Shelters the birds who work among the weeds.
They say the owner of the farm is dead
Yet every year the crops are harvested.

# *Harriet Gray Blackwell*

## "DELIVER ME FROM THE HORN OF THE UNICORN"

Deliver me from the horn of the unicorn.
Since I was born that hollow spear of shell,
half light, half pearl,
has haunted me;
closer than the skirl of life,
closer than sleeping, or weeping,
closer than love.

I saw the nimble-footed creature move
with my mother, Eve, upon his back;
he tossed his mane, she tossed her hair,
and their rapport was such they seemed one being.

He took her where the apple grew,
there she found the serpent, too,
and after one small bite of crimson-coated fruit,
she knew, she knew.

Innocence, now lost
as mango blossoms under frost
made her, my flesh, a stranger.

Danger prickles me, her daughter,
danger bright as sparkling water
wearing down a citadel . . .

There never is a warning bell,
no hoof crushes forest fern,
yet constantly I see
the shadow cast by a horn of pearl and light.

Then I tremble, then I know
that should it touch me, sound my name
even though I walked in snow
a sudden flame
would burn my heart to ash.

## *Frederika Blankner*

### THE ADORATION OF THE MAGI KINGS
Leonardo da Vinci

I was alone in an Uffizi room,—
Haven of templed beauty and of peace,—
Loving through ageing gray of twilight's gloom,
In lingering communion, each fair grace
Of Vinci's *Adoration,*—still a dream:

Through underpainting figures dimly seen
And then emerging as one's heart knew more,—
Faces of seraph beauty, hands that mean
All of our human groping blind beyond;
And this a shadow of the perfect whole,
Known only to the Master, lost to us
Forever.

—A Presence in the room—
The dull brown tints flowed deeper into gold
Or burst into rich panoplies of rose
Aflame and lyric azure, cypress green.
The chargers reared and panted with a breath
Snorting through silent pigment. Tenuous
The dreaming lip of shepherd trembled real:
Lifted, the ghost-like hand became ideal
Hellenic chasteness fused with Florence fire.

The Infant smiled and blessed, the Mother smiled,
Wisdom adoring prostrate at their feet.
This was not painting: this was life more real
Than granted to us creatures of the earth.
This was not painting: this was the ideal.

Then sudden darkness; I was left alone.

I have gone often to that haunted room,—
Dearest to me of all earth's solitudes,—
Seeking to know again the finished art:
Always the underpainting dimmed and brown;
Memory alone kindles the light beyond.
That perfect vision—had it been a dream?
Or had devotion moved the Master's soul
Once to reveal his plan complete and whole?

## *Robert Bloom*

### THE SNIPER

Lonely, he waits for the lonely kill,
devouring his fill
of breviaries, manuals. At arms,
he thinks how arms of trees
are greater, how his knees
will knock as he says his charms,
buttressed against the bole—
how the target will rise, creeping,
red drawers over the knoll.
At times he will even try sleeping.

Best, there is nothing at all

to be angry for—not the pall
of dark ash drifting down
where he got away from the town,
for the town was only a cause—
nor the old woman who bled,
nor the scarified captain's laws
(hadn't the young girls fled?) —
and how should he rage on a branch,
he, who knew how to be staunch?

*Our Father, Which Art On Our Side,*
*set my sights, but not too wide . . .*

Yet once more, Father, I trespass
against Thee, for Thy Name's sake.
In the hour of our death, I break
Thy bread, dismiss Thy mass.
Yet once more, Father, we contain
each other. Yours the power to restrain
me, mine to restrain You. Let us pray,
Father, and set my hand this day.

## *Hazel Bowers*

### EARTH-INHERITED

The meek cling and crawl,
grass their security;
meekly they mingle with worms,
crumble to dust:
They who inherit the earth
by earth inherited.

The bold glitter with sun,
stride the stars,
uprush the gusty wind,
crack the crystal of the sky,
clang the iron gate of Mars.

Stricken with earth,
though their blind bones
are carrion for the dust,
their vigor rips earth's bitter crust
and arrows toward the sun.

## *Charles A. Brady*

### KEEPER OF THE WESTERN GATE: FOR D.J.D.

There'd been an Irishman somewhere along the line.
That, and his First Ward tongue, made one forget
That the old man had been Indian all the time,
A Keeper of the Western Gate even as
His Onondaga brothers keep the Dream.
Barring a phrase thrust in here and there for fun,
He hadn't spoken Seneca in years –
Not since the Great War where it was his job
To send over field telephones at Château-Thierry.
(To confuse the German listeners, that was.
The French used Bretons and the English Cornishmen
Until someone remembered that the Boche
Had written all the grammars in those tongues.
Not for Seneca, though. Seneca had been professor-proof,
Even Herr Professor-proof.
The trouble was it took two Senecas,
One sending, one receiving, and there weren't

That many Senecas to go around.
At least, not for long.)

He'd kept that other Western Gate as well as any brave.
Because he'd lost an arm in doing so,
There was a medal in his dresser drawer
Among the fish-lines and the cartridge-waddings.
He didn't keep much. But he kept those ragged ribbons
As carefully as his kinsman Red Jacket once
Had kept General Washington's gift of a Silver Eagle.
In the coffin there was no doubting the Seneca blood:
Nose, eye-sockets, cheeks—it made good bones, too.
What else was there, besides the Iroquois?
He didn't know himself except to say,
And I was the only one who ever listened:
*Neh-ko, gah-gis-dah-yen-duk.* That is:
There were other council fires here before ours got lighted.
So there were. Eries –
They gave their name to our Lake, those men of the Cat.
Algonkians. Woodlanders. Who knows the old tribes now?
Right back to the bronze-faced hunters with their lances
Who tracked the giant elk and beaver down,
Down from the Asian north across the land bridge
While, year, by year, the chill ice-field retreated.

You had one "moccasin story," I remember,
Warm winter-shod and told in winter only
So that they would not waken:
Them totem-beasts. Also the lilliputian –
A word you did not know, but what else can I use here?—
The *oo-nees-heh-loon-eh-ah.*
Or is this Mohawk, not Seneca? No matter.
Your mother's mother was a Mohawk girl.
At any rate, the little folk who beat
Their water-drums so loud in spring and fall,
Which are the haunted times for Cattaraugus.

It was about a monster like a bear,
Only a greater Bear than one comes on these days.
I told it to a friend who knows such things.
He called it a folk-memory of a mammoth –
A mammoth-tooth is mounted in our museum.
You'll not tell it to your great-grandchildren now,
And they're far too few good stories left these days.
For a little while, perhaps, I'll tell it for you.

The Month-of-the-Branch-Women-Braid-into-Baskets was midway
When they called your friend the chaplain to your room.
Outside in the Indian dark, co-conscious, coeval,
Coaxial, too, with that frog-moist, soft night,
One last peeper, not yet bulldozed, piped your pibroch
In what I would call quite passable Seneca.
With a grin you said to the priest who understood:
*Don't waste your time with me, Mac, if you've other things.*
*I was never one to hold much with religion,*
I thought of Red Jacket's words to Erastus Granger,
In 1812, during Mr. Madison's War:
*Brother, if you white people murdered the Saviour,*
*Well, make it up yourselves.*
*We Indians had nothing to do with it at all.*

Yet you could tell what things in your hills were *oki,*
There where the deer still walk, in the morning black,
In the evening white, ghosts pacing delicately.
You never shot a rabbit you didn't eat.
You took a fish, one might say, with holiness.
The first drag on each cigarette was for the manitous –
Manitous plural, not one, as the white men say.

Old man, your blood flows in my first grandson.
Through you I touch those bones in the Black Rock ossuary.

I shape the fluted flint-tips one still scuffs
Aside on the beaches all around Buffalo.
I salute the turtles that swim in cold Diver's Lake.
In a sense, I am of your clan now, be it said,
For through your great-grandson we are blood-brothers
In the only way a man is adopted backwards.
It's true that no one really owns his land.
But there are degrees in being of the land.
Now I am of this land a little more.
And so, though we never talked very much in life,
In death, I, honorary Onondagan –
Since I, too, keep the Dream in a manner of speaking –
Commune with you, old kinsman, who keeps the Last
    Gate.

# *Joseph Payne Brennan*

## NEW ENGLAND VIGNETTE

Wind leaked through the clapboards;
In the icy garret, random flakes of snow
Skipped on the rafters. The house was a garrulous shell.
But he stayed on. There was nowhere else to go.

There were biscuits in the cupboard, turnips in the bin,
And a little tea locked up in a tin.
It wasn't much to eat on a winter's night.
It wasn't much. Even the rats grew thin.

The empty barn was full of dust and starlight,
No grain in the stalls, no hay in the mow.
Crickets, owls and spiders held the stage
With no clumsy interference from horse or cow.

He stood at the frosty window, every dawn,
And wondered what had happened to the land–
Why river birch were rooted in the orchard,
Why boulder walls were starting to disband.

It was too much for just one man, he told himself,
(Forgetting there never had been more than one.)
He stirred the stove, brewed a pot of tea
And sat to ponder what he might have done.

There was no final answer he could find,
And none, in fact, that he would ever know.
The wind sighed and the old house shook
And he stayed on. There was nowhere else to go.

## *Nancy Bruff*

### THE MIST MAIDEN

A cresting wave
Carves the Mist Maiden
Of spume and the wake
Left by a dream.
To see her once is forever,

In the moon shadow lying.

At the end, in the hour
Of our mortal peril
We will see her again
Drawing her nets
Woven of fog and time

In the surf shadow calling.

To hold us in her fragile space
Beneath the curve of a wave,
For a lifetime in a moment
Before we become what we must,

In the wind shadow drifting.

# *Helen Bryant*

## GRAFFITI IN TIMES SQUARE SUBWAY

They won't last, as those in
Pompeii did.
They'll be cleansed away
lethargically but completely
one dull mid-morning, but they
were written to be read and so I read them—
the least I could do, a
slight kindness, an acknowledgment
of someone's attempt to leave a record,
if only the usual four-letter words
scribbled in public places
or
a linkage of lovers like
Barbara and William or Jim and Judy, or
something even more pathetic.
Heil, Death! was one, which, given the environment,
was not really odd.
The clincher, in neat, scholarly cursive
on an iron pillar that trembled
at the train's passing, simply said
Manandgod.

## *Marion Buchman*

### THE DAY OF EMILY DICKINSON'S FUNERAL

Mr. Higginson came.
It was May.
A sunny day.
Marigolds illumed the lawn.

Inside the house
a glass of water embraced
violets.
On the piano
another tumbler of flowers.

Mr. Higginson looked into the box.
He regarded her domed brow.
"She is fifty-six
but looks thirty,"
he thought.

Her sister
had placed two yellow flowers
into her hands
to greet God with

## *Olga Cabral*

### POTATOE POEM

Small brown beasts with branched
stalked stalagmitic twiggy eyes:

potatoes that have lain too long
in a cupboard under brown
paper bags piled up like dry
winter's leaves.

Earth-skinned as hands of migrant pickers,
hibernating like a family of bears
in their dark kitchen-cave, they grew
long strands of tremulous sight,
fumbling in blind tropisms for
lost fields of light.

A thing as homely as a toad
yearns, yet can utter croak nor cry,
and so puts out pale lavender
and pearl green shoots
tipped with budding winks of brown
potato eyes.

Earth-creatures, was it you I heard
rubbing the door of my dream those nights
of waning winter, like secret wings
the sound of antennas rustling and growing,
tuned to mysterious call-letters of
potato Springs?

## *Melville Cane*

### HOUDINI

I

The papers said:
"Houdini Dead!"

Racing newsboys yelled:
"Houdini dead! Houdini dead!"
People read, smiled:
"Just another front
Page publicity stunt."
But Houdini was dead.

How can one get away with it, –
The box-trick, –
How can one fool Death?

No one could fix the committee,
An undertaker, chairman.
Dead men play no tricks,
But was he "playing dead"?
How could a dead magician
Put it over a live mortician?

They clamped him with manacles,
Shackled his ankles,
Clapped him in a case,
Strapped him to his place,
Locked the lid.
He did what he was bid.
They kept the watch by day.
They vigiled him by night
In the sputtering candle-light.
He never left their sight.

They bore him from the house,
They caged him in a hearse
(The hearse was framed in glass,
Was screwed with screws of brass,
And only light could pass).

They took him for a ride,

Captive, chained and tied;
They set him on the ground,
Coffined, fettered, bound, –
The damp November ground.
He made no sound.

The grave was dark and deep,
The walls were rich and steep;
They lifted him and lowered him,
They shoveled earth, a heavy heap –
A rising heap, a dwindling hole
A rabbi made a prayer for his soul.

II

Years ago, a mid-summer day,
Suddenly he stepped out on the shore,
Saugatuck, Long Island Sound.
Dropped his robe,
A bather,
Smiling, bowing, in the sun.
Incredulous ones
Peered within a packing case,
Felt for secret panels,
Tapped each side.
Strangers tied him, hand and foot and torse,
Hammered fast the top with nails of steel,
Roped and double-roped and tugged the knots.
A high derrick dipped,
An iron hook slipped,
Clinched the rope,
Pulled its dangling burden clear of land,
Plunged it in the waves.
Then, as it rose again, a swinging minute,
A swimmer stroked his triumph toward the bank.

To do the box-trick in water,

When the July sun is shining,
Is hard;
But, harder still,
On a cold November day
To swim through clay.

III

This was no mountebank
No spangled juggler
Of rubber-balls and billiard cues and lamps –
This was and is and ever will be spirit.
There is a legerdemain
Unsensed by mortal fingers,
A clairvoyance
The perishable brain
Is hopeless to attain.
There is a heart-beat of the spirit;
No one can time it.
There is a blood, a muscle, of the soul.
Lithe is the spirit and nimble
To loose the cords of the body;
Wiry and supple the soul
To slip the strait-jacket of the flesh.

IV

Out of an unbroken grave,
Above unheeding mourners,
Before the sightless eyes of conjurors,
Houdini rose
And lightly sprinted down an aisle of air
Amid the relieved and welcoming applause
Of those already there.

## *Maureen Cannon*

### TO A NEIGHBOR ON A RAINY AFTERNOON

After the shower the garden is steamy
And fragrant with earth-smells and such.
I'm longing to dance in the grass, but you'd see me . . . .
I don't (at least not very much).
Instead I go walking, umbrella-ed and staid
Down paradise paths that the raingod has made,
And nobody hears me, my laugh or my shout . . . .
Dear lady, wet lilacs are what life's *about!*

## *Margaret Haley Carpenter*

### ELEGY

Let the wind blow softly here;
 Let the shadows fall
Gently, gently, on this place
 Where the grass grows tall.

Here the moon will pour cool light
 In a silver flood,
Chilling with its crystal stream
 The once impatient blood.

Stars of snow will drift unseen
 When the nights are long,
And April rains sing heedlessly
 To ears now deaf to song.

In the silence, in the hush,
    Let the shadows fall.
Time, once reckoned by their length,
    Now matters not at all.

## *Mary Grant Charles*

### HIMSELF

Black is the early morning countryside
Black is the bog the market road runs through
Black is the Kerry cow he is driving before him
Black is the shawl that almost hides his woman's face
Oh, but himself is in a black, black mood the day.

Her smile surprises him; the sun routs the fog,
Turns black to brown, the brown to golden bog;
Her eyes green as the holly bush against a changing sky:
Och! The blackness of the world can never win it
Whilst God's green is in it!

## *Joseph Cherwinski*

### RIMBAUD IN AFRICA

His lids sprang wide to drink the morning scene,
He smiled, cursed, beat the spider on his thigh.
Sleep was a sowing and the crop was green
Until the light of morning seared his eye.
Now this– forever, this mad continent

Reaching for him with naked monkey hands,
Unwinding from his heart its cerement,
Tormenting him with Negro sarabands.

He heard the soft black footsteps coming in.
He closed his eyes against the tattooed breast.
He willed himself asleep. But no—the thin
Rank odor groping from its nest
Assailed him stronger than the dream of death.
The wet lips swallowed his and drank his breath.

## *Thomas Caldecot Chubb*

### GEORGIA AFTERNOON

The woods were full of birds
Swinging and singing from every branch of every tree,
Whole notes and half notes, their canticles without words
Poured out together in unrehearsed harmony.

There were towees, nervous and rasp-voiced. There was a plump
Rust-breasted, slate-backed robin, confident and bold.
I could hear a woodpecker's rattling attack on a stump.
Through the aisles of the longleafs a warbler slanted on gold.

A sparrow chipped, then fussed with a flutter of wings,
And another bird further away that I could not see or name—
Maybe a mockingbird enraptured with his rhapsodizing.
Then a cardinal whistled and flew by in his coat of flame.

Nor were the feathered ones all. As I indolently lay
And looked with eyes half closed at the broomsedge, the
waving broom,
A black fox squirrel paused and then bounded away.
His tail was a flaunted oriflamme, a proud plume.

In the distance, too, blurred, almost hidden in the haze
Of a half brown, half green hillside where no shadows ran
Was the bee's drone of cattle lowing. I could see them
graze.
Only they and the hum of the highway reminded me of
man.

This was Georgia on a winter afternoon.
The sun was warm, but the air was liquid and cool.
The air was refreshing and fine, but the sun had a boon,
The sun scattered largesse, lavish and bountiful.

Somewhere else, I knew, it froze and was chill.
Somewhere else was a blizzard with stinging snows blown,
But here the world was a draught you could drink to your
fill
From a brimming crystal goblet that you need not put
down.

## *Stanton A. Coblentz*

### CONSECRATION

It matters not if I, the priest, vanish from mind and sight,
So long as the temple columns rise, and the temple lamps burn bright.
It matters not if the driving crowd pass me with eyes of stone
So long as the altar scroll endures, and the psalm that I intone.

It matters not if I, the priest, fade in the swirling dust
So long as the Law and Light remain, and I never fail my trust.
For by the sparks our lives have lit, when form and name expire,
We serve the pulse of the timeless breath that fanned the stars to fire.

## *Leonard Cochran*

### ANCHORITE IN METROPOLIS

The mind's Sahara closes out
the steel trees of the city,
glassed-in mountains,
sounds of a concrete land.

Alone, I search my
proper country's bounds
to find a footprint in the sand.

## *Patricia Coffin*

### HIGH WIND

All night the wind
has been trying to get in,
rattling latches, shaking sashes, slamming shutters,
muttering
in the eves,
then rushing
the house and roaring in frustration down the chimney.

This morning
I opened the door.
As it tried to shoulder past I said:
"And what if I let you in
wind,
what would you?"

"I'd rinse your rooms with clean fresh air,
I'd shake your curtains, tumble your beds,
I'd sweep the house bare
of stale ideas and bacon smells,
of all things loose, lying pelmel like papers,
love letters old and new, manuscripts (both carbons and
original),
notes,
recipes on envelopes,
paper dolls and lists of things to do,
senseless habits and old memories too."

"No house could stand that much cleaning."
I shut the door leaving
the wind grieving
on the doorstep like a salesman gainsaid.

# *E. R. Cole*

## QUITTING THE ORIENT

Quitting the Orient with its sky-high
Delicious Himalayas, he sails west,
Pursuing answers and a handful of rest
To soothe an itching brain and feeble thigh.

He makes his blissful way now, all July,
Subjecting customs to his stringent test,
Uprooting verbs and planting them in his vest
With "What does this one mean?" and "That?" and
"Why?"

"Your sky," he says, "has made a friend of me,
"Slapping me on the back with its hot sun,
"Until I find that alder growing there";

And, blowing his final kisses toward the sea
He crossed, he waves his bones at everyone,
Jarring with laughter the missile-wounded air.

# *Mary Ann Coleman*

## ESCAPE

Father in the amputated wood,
trees are felled in the clearing for all our deaths.
Well deep, like a star, a reflection of light
gives back the sky on your flesh. You shine
so faintly that only I

can see in the daylight
the luminous peace you have made
in the knee deep forest your own length,
in the endless procession of coffins.

Later, the nightwatchman, checking the building for
    prowlers,
will move through rooms of bodies like Pharoahs,
safeguarding the diamonds and gold
that glint in his flashlight
around the ring fingers of corpses.
You will wear the shining of death
magnified, out of proportion,
till startled, he wakes the proprietor.
Embalmers hold their hushed conferences, examine their
    fluids,
but will not put out all your light.
Only the spade-wielded earth
will cover your ritual escape
until earth, checkered with graves,
opens, when silence cracks,
when cadavers rise and ignite
in the long burn of the sun.

## *Hasye Cooperman*

### NIGHT WITHIN US, DAY WITHOUT

The snow-white heron steps into the marsh.
The moment of his journey's end has come.
His silhouette against the glare is harsh,
Inscrutable and tentative and numb.

At this still point and in the mire our fates
Have intercepted time. Awaiting flight
We pass into the day. Our world abates.
Our "life dies sunward full of faith" in light.

The sky bird stirs, surrenders to the air,
Looks down upon the current's mirrored swift
Looks back upon his secret feeding lair
Then soars and spirals upward and adrift.

Night waits within each one of us. It lifts
Transmuted wings into the unknown rifts.

## *Annette Patton Cornell*

### THE WINE GOLD WEATHER

Her love went by in the gold, gold weather,
sun aslant on his dark, dark hair.
Her love went by with no sign whether
or not he saw her standing there.

Her love went by with a low, low whistle,
song on his lips that she could not know.
As rough the ground as sharp the thistle
for her who sees her dark love go.

Her love went by in the wine gold weather,
no sidelong look in his arrogant eyes.
Now she is lost in the gold, gold weather
with dark, dark dreams . . . and gold, gold lies.

## *Howard McKinley Corning*

### NEVER DENY A MOUNTAIN

Never deny a mountain, it will fall
Over your stateliest pace,
It will bow you down by the tall
Shadow upon your face.

Denial will make you little who should be great.
You will go lame to find
That lifted enormous weight
Plunging against your mind.

Days will come too early, nights too slow.
You will not see the length
Of earth beneath you for the sun's glow
On that granite strength.

Never deny a mountain: it is your power.
It is yourself unafraid
In that shaken importunate hour
When the earth's aid

Crumbles like ancient leaves, when the hands
Let go the beautiful flame;
And you cry to the mountain and the worldless lands
To speak your name.

## *Mildred Cousens*

### THE EGRETS

Three white egrets stood in the morning marsh,
motionless as figures stenciled upon glass,
their stemlike legs deep in the chill black water,
beaks all pointing across the open landscape
beyond the murky water, the wild morass.

Three white egrets, scarcely believable,
pure as Platonic virtues though less rare,
still as if waiting for a sign or signal
till from the tall pine grove a fourth one flew,
wheeling and circling in the sunlit air

over the others till they came alive,
lifted their beaks, fan-spread their folded wings,
forsook at last the dark primeval water,
wheeled and circled, then following their leader,
soared and flew in ever lessening rings
toward an unknown, yet somehow known horizon—

I called him courage for a human reason.

## *Betty Page Dabney*

### SANCTUARY

Let there be set apart
Close to the city's heart
An open place of green and quiet guise

For the slow fall of leaf on stone and water
And the reflected skies,
A shelter for the son of grief, the daughter
Of care. In the grave company of trees
Let them find ease,
In morning looks of children, rapt in play,
Whose brief, fierce joys and sorrows crowd the day.
Let the wheel turn aside there, and the hum
Of bargaining be dumb,
And let the refuge be
For the irresolute, the little-daring,
For him who walks the daily pavements, wearing
His complicated nature patiently.

## *Ann Darr*

### ONLY IN MADNESS

Only in madness would we conceive after noon is gone;
only in madness yank you into the universe
from nowhere one can get to easily, though we try.
                    Yet though the message is clear
that you are not coming at all,
and though I had not made a small nest of shredded papers
like our mouse, loss has formed a clot.
Hot tears are running my ink together, my red ink
where I record the deficit. I name you:
who unlike us gained death
without the broken bones.
    *In the ancient Bible I record that Will was born*
    *on a summer night in June, and died in hot July*
    *being grown to manhood only in his mother's mind.*

## *Mariana Bonnell Davenport*

### IN THE HOUSE OF HER MAKING

What can I do now but wait?
She has shut herself in the dark
And windowless house of her grief.
She has closed the door; she has turned the key.
One day she will open that door
To my love, and the words I would speak.
But need of that love is lost in her fear
Of my shaping it now into words
She is not quite ready to hear.
I must wait—and say nothing to her.
I must leave her there,
Alone in the house of her making.
With no other step on the stair.

## *Gustav Davidson*

### ALL THINGS ARE HOLY

All things are holy,
even the profane.

And whether we move
in illusion or reality,
if anything concerns us,
this already is its sanctification.

For there is nothing without its aura,
only it is for us to perceive it

and walk in the midst of it,
enchanted and haloed.

## *Mary Carolyn Davies*

### THE DAY BEFORE APRIL

The day before April
Alone, alone.
I walked to the woods
And I sat on a stone,

I sat on a broad stone
And sang to the birds.
The tune was God's making,
But I made the words.

## *Edward Davison*

### IN THIS DARK HOUSE

I shall come back to die
From a far place at last,
After my life's carouse,
In the old bed to lie
Remembering the past
In this dark house.

Because of a clock's chime
In the long waste of night,

I shall awake and wait
At that calm, lonely time
Each sound and smell and sight
Mysterious and innate—

Some shadow on the wall
When curtains by the door
Move in a draught of wind;
Or else a light footfall
In a near corridor;
Even to feel the kind
Caress of a cool hand
Smoothing the draggled hair
Back from my shrunken brow,
And strive to understand
The woman's presence there,
And whence she came, and how.

What gust of wind that night
Will mutter her lost name
Through windows open wide,
And twist the flickering light
Of a sole candle's flame
Smoking from side to side,
Till the last spark it blows
Sets a moth's wings aflare
As the faint flame goes out?

Some distant door may close;
Perhaps a heavy chair
On bare floors dragged about
O'er the low ceiling sound,
And the thin twig of a tree
Knock on my window-pane
Till all the night around
Is listening with me,

While like a noise of rain
Leaves rustle in the wind.

Then from the inner gloom
The scratching of a mouse
May echo down my mind
And sound around the room
In this dark house.

The vague scent of a flower
Smelt then in that warm air
From gardens drifting in,
May slowly overpower
The vapid lavender,
Till feebly I begin
To count the scents I know
And name them one by one,
And search the names for this.

Dreams will be swift and few
Ere that last night be done,
And gradual silences
In each long interim
Of halting time awake
Confuse all conscious sense;
Shadows will grow more dim,
And sound and scent forsake
The dark, ere dawn begins.

In the new morning then,
So fixed the stare and fast,
The calm unseeing eye
Will never close again.

. . . . .

I shall come back at last,
In this dark house to die.

# *Irene Dayton*

## STAGNATION

Green dying in green
this swamp feeds
away from river, hides.

Duckweed clings
to the oar, covers
the water dank, envelops
the swamp with
deepening scum. Cattails
reed-like lift heads
from green and
cankering brown.

The one determined—
like unto a wing's
fluttering movement
cuts into time
wrestles with his own
being; going as blue
heron who shivers in
sun, who for a moment
stands, feet poised
among black decaying
things, flaps
wings, feet stirring
undergrowth, beholds
other creatures
cowering down, then
circumspectly flees
this sink-
slippery green.

Sky tangles in trees
willows bend in grief
-I- becomes still.

## *Miriam Allen deFord*

### LETTER TO THE DEAD

Fable and figment of desire,
Our lesser Eden! On its fire
Ashes lie choked, the door is sealed,
The flaming sword that cannot yield
Posted before it.
Seven years
It has not yielded to my tears.
It never will. The lock stands fast.
Our present has become my past.

Seven Decembers gone to earth
Since we two drank to feast your birth,
And seven false-bright Junes since I
Stood helpless, mute, and watched you die.

Oh, is that true we once were told,
Each seven years the multifold
Cells of our being all are new,
And we changed creatures? Is that true?
Am I transformed? Am I not still,
By every impulse of the will,
That best beloved, that inmost friend,
Who in your death rehearsed my end?
I cannot make one into two—
It is that riven half of you
Endures a time you never knew.

Disaster writes our daily log,
Chaos is grown our household dog;
Facing catastrophe at flood,
We draft our history in blood.
Yet still, a traitor to my age,
I walk a hopeless pilgrimage,
And still with every endless year
Relive the time when you were here.

Too long, too long! Before the gate
The flaming sword stands obdurate.
O lost! and lost we who survive,
Too early born, too late alive!
Within my breast a beating stone
Remembers you: and I alone,
Lonely and lost, go forth to bear
The season's burden of despair.

## *Harriet L. Delafield*

### HILL SONG

The long way up the hill
Is often the best ascent;
The views more graspable—
The heart more still.
But take the short way down:
Racing the wind or ahead,
Chasing the bounding stone—
Your songs so blown
That when you look again
On near familiar scenes
Your words will still be ringing
Up there where you have been.

## *Albert De Pietro*

### CANDLE SONG

A gentle violence burns;
Dark distractions firm
And send their hostage shadows
To explore the flame
Our ransom breath sustains.

We clothe in shadow:
Unseen, the seeming stirs;
The touch of seeing blurs.

The air that burns
Is ours; we breathe back
Light. No flickers panic
Wax to candle hunchback;
No softer shadows turn
To ask, of love, the dark return.

## *Celia Dimmette*

### THE TURTLE

Drawn from the sea, the yard-wide turtle
Made the best of his plight on shore in thongs.
The men stood back, appraising the relic reptile.

Salt and red ashy mineral fogged the shell.
The persevering creature had winglike front
Flippers that moved, the toes grown together

And lacking some of the claws. His clamshell mouth
Opened, revealing the hollow, toothless and pink.

Barnacles grew on his back and he thrust forth
A dinosaur's neck, the hyoid apparatus
Therein pumping life for one with protruding
Eyes under lids half-closed.
Till having shot
The animal, they took the head, snapping
The bone who knew how long among
The kelp and sea lettuce. The creature lay
As an emblem the ocean cherished, and gave
For their use with loud arms. They turned
The sprawling four-footed primitive
In shell of time that did not matter.

Cutting around the sheath, exposed the weblike
Center with the heart like a peeled
Pomegranate near the strata of liver
And lungs that were coral-colored. How far life came,
They could not know, nor sea and earth remember.

## *Alfred Dorn*

### SNOWFLAKE

Here is a snowflake in my hand, like some
White Athens in the palm of history—
A moment's fragile Parthenon of frost.
It was the world-enfolding Hand, remembered
In marble by Rodin, that felt the empires
Falling like drops into oblivion.
It cupped the noon of Athens in its palm;

Its fingers knew the touch of Phidian snow
And spanned the crysalid of Plato's dream.

Perhaps this flake is some minuter Athens,
And I a god who holds it as it dies
To sudden dew. This molecule of world
May be dominion of a subtler nation,
Inviolate to our eyes.
                                        If atoms dream,
What kingdoms claim this melting star of snow!

## *Carleton Drewry*

### THE CELEBRANT OF SEASONS

Who had his way, who had his want
Of spring, deep-earth intoxicant,

Grim wayfarer beyond his will,
He strays about the woodland still

To haunt the autumn, gather grief
With the long wind the loosened leaf.

The hare and mole have learned to hide,
The field-mouse and the fox abide
Under the heel of winter's stride.

He stays alone to face the blight
On earth and flesh of appetite,

With slaken need, with senses shrunk,
With the last drop of summer drunk.

Bird without wing, beast without fur,
A naked thing, he sees the blur
Of change, feels the first cold occur,

Creep on the warmth that was desire,
An ash of bloom for every fire.

Yet he is rooted in his dearth,
And grown too toxic with the earth

To burrow down or beat above
That closing mother-trap of love:

The heart awaste in winter weather,
The withered wood, these grieve together,

Lost green of heart, gone green of bough,
Alike availing neither now.

## *Lora Dunetz*

### ON VISITING A EUROPEAN CATHEDRAL

Marvel more at the works of man
Than of God Who is by nature limitless
(Whose miracles are no miracle); for man, the artisan,
The poet, whose pain is his mortality, has
Raised his many mansions from his eloquent
Finiteness. From his half-perceived and endless
Root, spring living angels of granite
And marble. His captured visions, his artifice
Of moons and suns, his ornamented font
To catch the supreme flow, his tremulous

Thrust of arch and spire—all his confident
Travailed creations, release
God from Himself into the world's expanse
To manifest the conjoint circumstance.

## *Burnham Eaton*

### BLOW

At rest in darkness here in the night's unrest
I hear the brace and give of stout beams warning
walls, pegs, and brittle nails to hold the room
and roof steady against the thrust and boom
of things that move that did not move this morning.

"Only the wind," you say, but only the wind
can push the knob, can set the boards to creaking
like opened latches onto an open space
where something runs with heavy tread, without face,
in vast noisy silence without speaking.

It flung a hail against the window. It pinned
a spray of broken leaves caught in midflight
hard on the glass. They quivered and were away
singing a chantey of oceans of the air . . .
With the old house I ride the ridden night.

# *Charles Edward Eaton*

## THE TREE-FROG

I was kept awake nearly all night by the tree-frog
Which provoked a nostalgia almost too keen to bear:
It had something to do with revolution and the underdog.

A sound so insistent is very like the rebel
Who tries to conquer us by sheer compulsion:
The complaint of the put-upon has something similar to
tell.

I have a powerful nature in pursuit of pleasure,
Peace, good will, and I do not share
My time's contempt for passion balanced by strict measure.

And yet this aggression which is comparable to pain
Puts a cutting-edge on things, no doubt about it,
Making passion and balance themselves seem suspect or
inane.

The brutal thing about our life, in its broad sweep,
Is that these urgencies are ubiquitous and constant—
Another night the tree-frog will still be there, and I shall
sleep.

But if I play with form and feeling, I am also played
upon—
The tree-frog draws a bow across my nerves,
And I am raw with harsh and heartfelt music just before
dawn.

## *Richard Eberhart*

### EVIL

When I entertained evil
I played upon him as if he were good.
At my red banquet table
I set before him peppery food.

I thought he was king of the world.
His elegance, his subtlety
Were without question in my mind.
His sensibility was exquisite.

He seemed like a devil incarnate
But so much like my friends, myself,
That I recognized a hidden truth.
At a banquet table nothing offends.

We talked of the affairs of state.
Should one turn the other cheek?
The idea was that to lose face
Was a shame in being weak.

None thought to kill was bad.
The pictures of the lacerated Vietnamese
Were somehow not to be mentioned.
None thought that any here was obese.

There is a certain delicacy
In what to say at a dinner party.
The idea is to accept man as he is
And rejoice at eating hearty.

Now I opened a bottle of Rosé.

It was a symbol of relaxation.
We were all feeling well
And I offered a toast to the nation.

I said, let us drink to freedom.
This seemed brightly reasonable
As everyone around the table arose
In our state of hedonism.

We drank to the glory of our state,
None thinking this uncouth.
We drank to individual aims,
And to the complexity of truth.

Our guest, a ruler of the world,
Was delightful, polite. I saw his bloat.
He said that evil was the greatest good,
My imaginary bullet through his throat.

## *Deborah Eibel*

### THE KABBALIST

Because his madness had outgrown the world,
He asked the moon to magnetize his hand.
He died a fledgling, as a mystic should.
His transit levelled trees, made shadows stand.

The night he tunnelled winter-to-the-moon,
A distance saints and outlaws undertake,
Disciples wept. The scrutinist was gone:
A book would henceforth be an undragged lake.

No. Every night he came as passerby.
His mind an anchor, he transformed their minds
Into inverted boats. Moon-magnetized,
He mastered men and trees and birds and winds.

## *Jean Elliot*

### CONCH SHELL

That which I leave behind will never tell
how I have fared as this escalloped shell
proclaims the creature it caparisoned;
my skull, which, adamantine, garrisoned
five senses and a never-sleeping brain,
will preach to the beholder only pain
while any idiot, with eyes, can guess,
looking on this sea-sculptured comeliness,
how beauty moved attendant on that track,
instant and constant on the wave-hewn back.

Could I by choice—one favor granted me—
exchange eventual monstrosity
for so indicative a carapace
but must, so straitened, forfeit your embrace,
become, instead, incessant ocean's bride,
drifting forever with the sensuous tide,
I would not trade the tenderness I know
for dark uncertainty of undertow.

## *Richard Curry Esler*

### SONNET FROM THE PORTAGES

The northern lakes thrust loose green fingers deep
into the folded granite of this land.
I go up tree-screened water through a stand
of wedded spruce root-strapped against the steep
gray rock. The water moves in quiet swirls
behind my paddle, and the ripples round,
nuzzling the shore with a soft sucking sound.
White birch lean over with the arms of girls.
The air smells faintly of a sweet decay
where thin soil sweats under the fallen leaves,
building fecundity against the day
when seedlings lengthen as their rooting weaves
through sterile stone to crumble it apart
and vein the granite with a greening heart.

## *Vesta Nickerson Fairbairn*

### OLD HOUSEBOATS

Wave-borne no more nor landlocked yet
The anchored houseboats tug and fret
At weathered pilings, hawsers, chains,
And feel the surge of tides' refrains
Along the marshland's channeled stream.
The salt winds blow and sea gulls scream
Above the cattails, grass, and sedge
Whose creeping roots will shortly wedge
The restless boats in drifted sand
And fetter them to alien land.

## *Norma Farber*

### *FEE-BEE!* SANG THE CHICKADEE

Scissors, a golden pair,
shear me awake with shut-
and-open song-edge. I rise
to a tempered sun cutting,
cutting, cutting fine air
with blades of bird-throat fire.

Yet sound he sleeps, that son,
my mother-in-law's. Longsince,
he sang me wide to my life.
I lean against his in-
out breath. Its passage rends
me, knife of phrase of knife.

## *Jessie Farnham*

### PENANCE

I filched a fragment from Eternity,
I thought no one will miss one little minute,
And then I learned it was gigantic time,
That over the world there had occurred within it
New birth, new death, new sorrow and new joy,
The million things a minute can destroy,
The million things a minute can give life:
All these I severed with my thieving knife.

And I was frightened and said I would return

The valued minute for I had time to burn;
But it was easier spoken than it was done,
The earth had moved that minute around the sun
And I had broken a link in Eternity's chain,
For I had murdered as surely as if I had slain.

And now for penance there races within my mind
A giant clock that is always a minute behind,
And everything my heart has wished within it,
Always falls short by just one little minute.

## *Ruth Feldman*

### NAZARÉ

I heard the town before I saw it,
Left the fogbound car, kicked off my shoes,
And struck out for shore.

A rhythmic chant drew me
Where mist-blurred fishermen
Strained at their ropes,

Stretched nets along the beach,
And looped them pole to pole
In drooping arabesques.

Dark-kerchiefed women squatted patiently,
Waiting for the sea to give a sign,
Or poked with sagging hope through the scant catch.

Enveloping gray dissolved

And brilliant boats bloomed out of sand,
Their blindeyed prows upflung.

Scarlet and silver-gilt,
Improbable flowers on the drying-racks,
Gutted fish glittered in the sun.

For begging hands that day
The haul was lean
As the sea's begrudging yield.

Their babies grafted on strong hips,
The women strove with wind
And took their hunger home.

## *Annette B. Feldmann*

### THE GLASS CHINA CLOSET

Let the wind flail the rain
Into a tattoo of remembrance
*A falcon's eyes are hooded in sleep.*

Let the wind flail the rain . . .
the eyes of my parents follow me
I make my first baby steps, turtle-like
through a long corridor,
into a room where a huge walnut china closet
holds a black brass buffalo—
a green toy turtle, wound up moves slowly,
aping its movements, I toddle along.

Suddenly, I see a Turkish hookah,

a rainbow-colored paper weight
and rows of finely cut Bohemian glass.
I watch my father, looming tall, he says;
"At last, the child walks."
Let the wind flail the rain
psyche is a world in which ego is contained,
The falcon's eyes are hooded in sleep.

## *Thomas Hornsby Ferril*

### CANTER THE HORSES, PLEASE

Country boy, I see you with your lantern
Swinging your giant shadow against the trees,
You're climbing the chokecherry draw where I'm
 always repeating
 . . . *canter the horses, please* . . .
. . . words not making sense to a companion,
Might there be one, nor sense to mare or whip,
Some ritual like a child's I start and stop
With turgor of my lip against my lip.

I won't dismount, explain. You're someone else
Walking the same draw now, left shoulder west.
Is the world beautiful? The lantern light?
Something to chokecherry your throat's addressed?

Let there be ritual, sir, if you return
To this dark valley, warring years behind,
Something you started to say, don't understand,
And love and half recall and hope to find.

## Margaret Fishback (Antolini)

### CHRISTMAS PAGEANT

The third-grade angels, two by two,
March in, their cardboard wings askew.

A kindergarten shepherd skips;
A halo from its mooring slips.

The oriental kings, all three,
Wear Momma's costume jewelry,

While spotlights from each ribboned wreath
Accent the braces on their teeth,

And wise men, from the upper classes,
Look very wise in horn-rimmed glasses.

## Ruby Fogel

### $E=MC^2$: A SESTINA PROVING THE EQUATION

WHIRLWINDS, WORLD-WHEELS, once set in motion
can have no ending nor beginning:
        must all run clockwise out of Time—
        from some unknown and mystic place;
no counter-clockwise path returning
ever again to primal night.

As day-blind bats awake by night
to stir wing-circled winds to motion,

stars float through full clouds, overturning
small drops of light: the day's beginning
streams from a waterfalling place
that turns great sun-wheels around with Time.

But now the curvature of Time
presents a problem to the night—
confronts it with the timeless place
whirling before this patterned motion:
what was it like in the beginning,
when wandering worlds *began* their turning?

Perhaps a new concentric turning—
a sudden spiral-point in Time
(when *"Let there be light"* proclaimed beginning
and *". . . there was light"* concluded night)—
Time started on its clockwise motion
from that perpetual starting-place.

It must be circular . . . a place
of whirlwind; always must be turning;
and spinning from a grand commotion
the constant, coiling wheel of Time.
A whirlwind's core is calm and night;
a central Calm was The Beginning.

Now far beyond that first beginning,
light-years from that primeval place
tomorrow circles from tonight—
from the calm Source of Time and turning,
that wound the clock-wheels of all Time
and set wild worlds in wheeling motion.

*. . . and Time still curves . . .* conformed to turning
like space or night. In curving motion,
each place of ending brings beginning.

# *Edsel Ford*

## LOOKING FOR SHILOH

Looking for Shiloh on a country road
To keep its appointment as the sign had promised,
We forded two streams where, coming out,
The car shed water like a running bird.

What this Shiloh might be, we couldn't guess.
But, crossroads or country church with tongueless bell
And stones leaning over tongueless dust,
It had a poetry about its name.

Pursuing Shiloh like a rhyme for silver,
We clung to the clay road cutting through the woodland
Till the sudden sight of two immobile crows
Trounced on the brake, and I reversed the car.

"Decoys," you said, and I in my chagrin
Fumbled with the gearshift. Out of the brush
Stepped the hunter, bearing a handmade crow-call,
Grinning a snaggled grin.

We asked how far
It was to Shiloh, as if we'd stopped to ask.
—He didn't know, he'd never been on through:
And waited, sky-eyed, for us to go.

Driving interminably, whittling the road to nothing,
Finding no thing which bore the mystic name,
We turned around and came back to the highway,
Wondering if the sign had been a decoy

Or if time had toppled all that was addressed
Along the road. Perhaps under the tangle
of thorny tomorrows will lie the poems which
We pointed to today but never found

Because, like Shiloh, they were in too deep.

## *Jeanne Robert Foster*

### THE YOUNG YEATS

No one was ever young as Yeats was young,
Who met with the old gods on misty strands
That bordered upon magic seas.
There was no other poet whose youth time
Was an enchantment and a spell:
No other to whom hills and waters spoke
In voices murmuring an ancient tongue.

No one was ever young as Yeats was young,
For when he walked the roads,
All men drew back a little as he passed
Feeling a difference though they could not know
He rode the wind and the rebellious tide.

No one was ever young as Yeats was young—
Nor old, for then the Masker dropped the Mask
And the wise artificers of the gods,
Gave him the likeness of a Golden Bird
Beaten by goldsmiths of Byzantium,
And changed him to a symbol in the mind.

## *Nelchen Foster*

### MADONNA

It wasn't that eventide
Which gave her the greatest joy,
When bearing a lilied rod
The angel prophesied
Christ's birth, nor when her boy
Died and arose a God.

But luminously she smiled
Remembering, loving best
That once, in her embrace,
To the haloèd child
The moon was his mother's breast,
The sun was his mother's face.

## *Siv Cedering Fox*

### NIGHT IN THE ADIRONDACKS

We left the lawn and the telescope (line
it up with an X in the middle of the moon)
to walk down the road in search of whatever
vixen or he-wolf (in a trap?) or pup is
yapping at his first feel of death or dying.

But what could we find on a road surrounded by
trees and mountains that toss and confuse
the sound? So we walked, in silence, each in
a separate universe of fumbling, through our art
or science, for whatever stars know, and trees.

For there is a kenning in that canine howl
that pulls us. Although there is no instrument
to X the spot of pain and no lenses ground
to reach the origin of sound, there is something
we must undo in the dark—that claims us.

## *Marilyn Francis*

### THE NURTURING OF NEMESIS

The nurturing of nemesis becomes a pride
Of subtle indecisions
Rehearsed and hung inside
In double dialogue of threat and counterthreat.
The whirlpool of a mind so occupied
Can grow a black narcissus;
In fascination soon forget
All beauty which does not reflect
The same dark flower.
The inner view cannot forever be denied,
The nurturing of nemesis becomes a pride.

## *Florence Kiper Frank*

### ANNETTE IN HEAVEN

She has loved always
Glitter of light.
Will she be desolate
In the large night?

Or will the angels
Bring there to bloom
Merciful candles
To whiten her room!

Will there be down
For the little gold head
That in justice should sleep
Upon nettles instead?

She has walked always
Clad in the grace
Of quick-glowing velvet,
Of ermine and lace,

And harshly indeed
Would her sinful heart fare
If they should give her
Homespun to wear.

She has no hardihood
Yet to endure
The rigors of God
That would render her pure.

She has forgotten
The prayers she must pray
Whose lips have had only
Bright words to say.

Her feet that are languid
Would bleed in the bone
Should she go barefoot
The way to the Throne.

May Peter abate
Her penance awhile,
Breaking his heart
On her innocent smile.

And may the dear Mary,
Tender of dole,
Grant her one lover
Her bed to console.

## *Helen Lovat Fraser*

### THE LEAVES

So there are blowing the dry leaves,
Swirling over the road while the grave trees bend.
O! there are blowing the rootless ones of the world,
The ones the winds play with, kick around
Until they crumble into powder.
The leaves—and all other rootless husks of things
That are blown by winds, drenched by the autumn rains—
Dry into dust or moulder into soil.

You who still have your roots would do well to remember
The dark winds and the leaves and the rains of November.

## *Louis Ginsberg*

### FAMILY BARBECUE

The garden could not soak up all the tensions.
Roses could not subpoena all the rancors.
And though the forgiving sun poured down its warm
And generous admonitions, the family clotted
In little knots of feuds about the grill.
The children, though, kept milling around in games,
Unheeding shadows not cast by the sun.
Aside from lovers tangled in themselves,
Uncles and aunts and cousins picnicked in
Assorted quarrels and litter of regrets.
Questions like "Why don't you ever write to me?",
Wavered in air and scattered in the grass.
Some relatives hid different envies under
Pretense of gayety in a glass of beer,
Or over hot dogs, they warmed their old resentments.
Aunt Mildred was vendetta in dark dress;
Aunt Sadie was miasma in green sweater.
And Cousin George, who floated all his years
Aloft by loans, drenched with his many drinks
His wounded pride. In drooping Uncle John,
Who disappeared into his many griefs,
Only his roving eyes survived his life.
And there was seedy and ragged Uncle Sam,
Dressed in his old and tattered homilies.
To talk with bitter Cousin Will was like
A dialogue as with sulphuric acid . . .

. . . .

The ghosts of their grandparents were distraught
At the frustration of their hopes to see
The family in its annual ritual
Of juggling enmities and balancing
Hostilities around the barbecue.

# *Harold Willard Gleason*

## VANISHED CONVOY

—Gone, all gone, those schooners with names like singing—
*Thetis, Lavolta, Georgietta, Rosella* and *Lenore*—
Far from the sheltering port that bred them winging
Out, to return no more . . .

Gone, too, the drudging tug that down the river
Squired them sturdily, surely into the turquoise bay,
Watched them spread sails and vanish—now, forever—
Out past the headland gray . . .

Yet sometimes on moonless nights when sea-mist, sweeping
Into the pine-fringed passage that leads to the rotting piers,
Blankets the town, a tugboat captain, sleeping,
Starts as he dreams he hears

Laughter and shouts of lads long turned to dust—
Eager, the voyage before them, enraptured at safe returning—
Rattle of rigging, creak of hawsers, and thrust
Of a tug's propeller churning . . .

(Ellsworth at one time was quite a lumber port, though now there is no shipping here. Names of the schooners are those of real schooners of 50 years ago, all from this or neighboring ports; and Ellsworth's towing down the Union River to the bay was done by one valiant little tug, now gone, the *Little Round Top*.)

## *Ryah Tumarkin Goodman*

### ANCESTORS

I am heavy with ancestors:
Headstones on my head,
Epitaphs in my eyes
That no one reads,
Dead fingers
Strumming on my heart.

I am heavy with origins:
Roots deepening,
Digging into me
As into a grave.

This weight I wear lightly,
But the weight of the unborn
Buries me.

## *Katherine Gorman*

### BLESSED, ALL WHO DIE BUT ONCE

Like a bird, a circling thing, he comes
The boy of love, the wing-heeled ghost.
He soars green continents,
Full of journeys, monuments, zodiacs,
Ancient roads and cataracts.
Again I am dug up like buried bone.

My silver, grown rust-thick, is taken down,
I hammer out the eaves for the gold eclipse.
Morning spangles through the singing thatch.

Bamboo thin, magic tangled in your hair,
I wake to pipe you off to Zanzibar,
Athens, Bengal, Martinique,
As wild things go like elephants to die.
I walk ahead of you and don't look back.

Trinkets come from Dublin or Bombay,
Messages from Mozambique, from Rome.
In my cupboard of secrets I hoard the key
And your last look, as something left behind,
Words not said, not written:
　　　　Stand in wait, Love, where you are.

## *Darcy Gottlieb*

### THINGS THAT DIE IN THE CITY

Things that die in the city
die a different death
from those in woods
or at land's end.
The leaf falling
on pavement gets no ritual
from a welcoming earth
the bird collapsing
in a gutter
is innocent of last crescendo
of heart against grass
or stinging sea.

wild things need to mate
with wildness in their dying.

## *Lillian Grant*

### ADOLESCENCE

Silver stream
trickling over bedrock,
yesterday he braved your swelling current
and found a mermaid dreaming
of lupine on the hill.

Today he stands
alone above that deep ravine
where spring and sudden summer meet —
small boy again, down at the river
crushing wild blue flowers in his hand.

## *May Gray*

### THE DAY SUMMER ENDED

I

Susan,
for a long time
I have been standing where we played
(summer-children on the beach

near the great sea-wall — now look at it —)
standing where we stood, when, above
the heart's terror, above the roar and echo
of the squall that spiralled in,
we heard our father's voice.

Only God knows

why, and how,
in that uneven race with sand and wind and water
over, under, and round about us,
a solitary wave housed me on the shore and,
sea-borne, folded you in sleep.

Did you see them warring with the waves?
Did you hear the curlew's keening cry?
Oh, Susan, were you frightened too,
or was there time?

## II

Father . . .
and father . . . I called to him . . .
He seemed not to hear; painted day and night
like a man with four hands and too much time.
Hoping, hoping a little, perhaps,
that mother would notice
your almost breathing beauty in the frame
(instead of staring with empty eyes
at the water day and night.)

But mother had no time

to look at anything except to memorize
the splashes of the tide;
the light and shadows in the air.

And father,

asserting a final emptiness and need for you
to be remembered, and loved with another kind

of love, gave you to the world. The portrait,
like a vision bears a wound too deep to see, as
you smile down from the museum wall, safe — ?
(I never have learned what is safe
or unsafe) above the ocean's highest, wildest
tide. It's still there, lovely as in memory,
to break our hearts again.

III

Burned out from all that fury and no higher than
my hand, these waves, as if atoning after all
these years, are rainbow-colored and warm as
a flame at my feet. If only they had melted
my mother's frozen heart.
Not knowing
what to do with time she lost the days —
All except that last one when she gathered
her affairs about her close as grief,
and walked, then ran out of reach
into the rocking tide. She said she saw you
in a green wave.

IV

All is changed now to a white peace. The snow
is falling, falling.
Your places, as narrow as the old-new sleds
you loved are filling up with snow like a blanket,
and both of you so still.

## *Bernard Grebanier*

### TO A CHIPMUNK WHO BUILT A NEST IN THE ATTIC OVER MY BEDROOM

You've heard my step and, panic-stricken, scurry
above the plywood ceiling where you've made
your family's house against the winter's flurry—
then halt before your young ones' nest, dismayed.
I feel your frightened heart-beat's throb; you bid
your mate cease rolling nuts across the floor
to where the pile of provender is hid;
he listens too as I unlock the door.

It matters not I plan toward you no ill,
and gladly yield you room beneath my roof—
I am the unseen power girt with dread.
So I, though all about me God grants proof
of His immeasurable love, grow chill
at but the echo of His silent tread.

## *Lisa Grenelle*

### POINT, COUNTERPOINT

Rioters rip the belly of the block
gyrate
in a cacophony of hate: white helmet,
copper muscle
tangle and tussle, moan and curse.

People divide down the middle.

Anger
loosed from a bottle struts the walk
roaring
an intent to eliminate all but like-sons.

Across the street, behind quiet trees
tennis players
leap and laugh about the courts.
White shorts
edged in copper tones (natural
and sun induced)
*Your serve . . . love all . . .*

## *Louise D. Gunn*

### BETWEEN NOW AND NO MORE

The air-letters (thin and fragile as
tissue thoughts) keep on coming,
dropping in multiple on my desk
like white-washed leaves in sepulchre.

What shall I write back
to a mind dying young?
What wind of the world
has dried its growth, so
fringed flower may wilt and
red cheeked fruit be lost
for always and always?

What wind of the world? What wind?

Let me battle with the wind, I cry;

but too late, I am, to fight the wind
that punishes the first-bloom petal;
too weak, I am,
too ignorant of winds and the will of winds.
. . . The letters cease.
All I can do, at last, is to wait,
wait and listen,
while the winds blow
and the will of the wind takes it will. . . .
I listen for the drop of onion-skin letters
thin as the margin of now and no more.

## *Lawrence Gurney*

### CARLSBAD CAVERNS

Like leaves of some black tree in Hell
Stirred by a Stygian evening wind,
The bats in rustling clusters fell
From sapless trunks of marble arch
In billowing, sightless waves,
Like leathery autumn leaves before a wind
As dank and cold as Charon's breath.

Warm in the lazy evening light,
The cowpoke sat against a ledge
And watched the billowing cloud,
As black as his own smoke was white,
Pour from the mountain's shadowy lee
As if some laboring El Paso freight
Had stopped beyond the hill.

## *Oliver Hale*

### THE HISTORY

It is quiet with me now,
aging. Desire is no more,
like the boys at marbles who
in my mind we once were.

What the eye sees is my last
enjoyment now violence
is done, and only a boy's ghost
is a mindful presence.

Him I remove with his games
to his far playing; yet out
of horizons he will sometimes
come, all in his child's state.

Then faces intrude; and playmates,
parents, teachers lost in years,
swarm like returned moons whose lights
are bright as present stars.

There was an old street, still slum,
where innocence died; there boys
turned men, and the world like flame
roared in awakening eyes.

Not in solitude I grew
but companionably, found words
sharp as foxes made nights gay,
and love moving inwards.

Gone are early friends, faces

shrewd and young, their hopes like stars
and all their fixed purposes,
fables between two wars.

Quieted now, their presences
like old thoughts command the mind
at moments, and their faces
are water touched by wind.

In that sea my image blurs, too,
where only seen clear are your love,
late friends and moderate joys, and the sky
falling in from above.

## *Amanda Benjamin Hall*

### A GIRL NAMED HELEN

Think of her as a child you might have known,
    evoke her gentle, innocent and good!

Where grandeur was a commonplace, her eyes
    saw marble temples fleshed in Aegean light,
and sun-burned shepherds with their fleecy moutons
    grazing in dizzy pastures next the skies,
where land fell off in peril to the sea,
    pure indigo with waves as white as cotton.

Through hall and colonnade she heard the rumors
of war and daring deeds beyond those shores,
    saw spear and breastplate ever at the ready!
As harp-strings plucked, resound beneath the hand,
    *her small self shook* . . . The beauty of her face,

so cherished in a world where much was wrong,
    stunned the beholder; strong men found it heady
and blushed like boys to tie her sandal thong.

And one adoring slave, a clever fellow,
    carved pretty toys for her and proud triremes
of olive wood. On classic afternoons.
    at ebb of tide when ocean pools were shallow,
with a child's delight in anything that floats,
    she launched a fleet of little wooden boats.

## *Leona Hamilton*

### "CRAZY WOMAN"

Stunned and shunned, she
Hovers the road-edge.

Her grin is toothless;
Her stride is gypsy;
But in her eyes are
Caravans of song.

From their yards
The women fling stone-glances.
Through leprous lips,
Babble of coiffures and cadillacs.

Scraping among dead leaves,
I find the geranium
She has planted.
It is the first to bloom —
Touching my garden to tambourines!

## *James Hargan*

### CORINTHIAN PILLARS

Remember the time we fled the college library?
Leaving behind the stale smell of books and students,
we hid stiff shoes behind Corinthian pillars
to wander barefoot, pagans in April rain.
Remember the high hill
with anonymous wild flowers that we named
with names of children who might some day be ours?
That day, for the first time, we thought
we might as well kiss.
Of course, you do not, must not remember
for long ago you married somebody else
and, I am told, have numerous children
all properly shod and with Christian names.
While I, dank with repetitious April,
lean against Corinthian pillars
and stare at the rainy blur of a high hill
that is not worth the toil of climbing again ever
just to stare at nameless wild flowers.

## *Dorothy Harriman*

### BOUND WATER

In Squaw Creek now no water flows:
The winter sunlight mean and thin,
Shadows those zero-tinctured snows
Drifted across the glen.

No cinnamon fern, no maidenhair,
No alder leaf and not one wild
And water-hungry wood mate there,
Now that the creek is sealed.

Only the wind and a sober fastness
Over the blue brash cold—no sound—
Only the ice, unwilling witness
Of water hushed and bound

## *Marjorie Hawksworth*

### AFTER WINGS

AFTER WINGS
had beaten her to the ground,
Leda, released by the holy swan
lay stunned but serene.
White birds gliding through her blood

solemnly sought the shell
where their hollow bones were filled
with the marrow of man. Leda knew
that the egg she laid
was purple as hyacinth;
that was all Leda knew.

That it sheltered a Helen
whose moulting from immortality
would burn the far plains
of Troy with feathers of flame—

unaware.

## *Dorsha Hayes*

### THE DANCE IS A FLASH IN TIME

Word-forsaker, motion-maker,
    rhythm-riding dancing girl!
Surging urge in leap or whirl,
        joy-expending,
        life-commending,
taut and limber, limp and firm!
    Flung flesh in a blood-beat swirl!
    Sun-swivelled in looping line!
Body a hoop and a shaft and a loom
weaving a vanishing filigree form
        earth-transcending,
        time suspending!
            Soar!
            Soar!
The dance . . .
            is ending.

## *B. A. Heimbinder*

### ASSIGNATION IN AUSTRALIA

Lunajane, incline upon
The wave-length of your Terrajohn,
And split the astral pile in two
That pressures me away from you.

For I am flamed to soar tonight
Where Alph Centauri spins his light,

And solar spear and cosmic dart
Shall forge no bar against my heart.

So gleam your gown to guide my flight
With shimmering micrometeorite;
Twinkle your hair with trails that fly
From galaxies and nebulae,
And launch me with a megakiss
To spark our astro-genesis.

## *Brodie Herndon*

### THE EXCAVATOR

Careless alike of bear and where the ant is,
The pendulous head rises above its prey.
Like some enormous, garden praying mantis,
It strikes, then strikes again; and rises to sway
And swing upon its double neck of cable.
Dribbling dinner of roots and rocks and ferns,
It mixes shale and marl upon its table
With sweet and ancient forest loam; and turns
Indifferently a tree between its teeth.
Crunching through the bones of any hill
The clanking, grattling glutton feels beneath
Its mantis maw, it presses down until
It has persuaded lion and little toad,
No hill should rise above the level road.

# *Ruth Herschberger*

## SERGEI

*I said: I fear and resent men.*
*He said: I'm not a man, I'm a flower.*

Sergei's a flower—
  What a flower!
    A broncho of a bloom.

Carnation, rose,
  A soft primrose,
    Chrysanthemum, or whom?

Sergei's a bower,
  What a bower!
    A grapevine of delight.

Sergei's a pose,
  A yellow rose,
    A stallion in the night.

# *Miriam Hershenson*

## KADDISH FOR MY FATHER

(Prayer for the Dead)

My father, who gave me the curl of my hair,
And the twist of my mind;
The spirals of my thinking,
And the circles of my love;

(Too early planted in death—
A poet's early dying.)

Lacerated with an old wound,
Why do I call to you now
Healed decades later,
Whose clothes were not torn at your dying?

(Too early planted in death—
A man too early dying.)

Graduate of ghettoes, connoisseur of exiles,
Who taught you Shakespeare and freedom?

(Too quickly planted in death—
My life absolves your dying!)

## *Lois Smith Hiers*

### CHINA BOUND

I, too, thought of digging for China—
One or another of those bonanza days
Cheered by a startled cock, his hark-hosanna
Rivalling the incandescent praise

Of dew's mute cymbals, I airily laid claim
To early passage. As moles go, I would go:
Part the earth as sailing ships part foam
En route to dragon country. China, I knew,

Hung walled and upside-down, defying space—
Peacocks paraded, mandarins in gold—

Green robes invoked twin deities of peace
And war, in a land where Yin-yang ruled.

One or another day, I thought that long
And legendary trek, but always a bird
Sang me a journey here; or a fish sprang
Free of the waterbrook and thought disappeared.

Perhaps, from Time's burning, it was better to keep
Enchantment whole, to never have lost or have found
That Middle Kingdom; better to dream a tall ship
Than to wake, China bound.

# *Hyacinthe Hill*

## ALL'S RIGHT!

(On having seen the photograph of a living 18-week-old fetus shown inside its amniotic sac.)

How good
to hold
the seed of a child
inside,
asleep, like a grape on a stem,
in a skin room
where one can send
through artery and vein
food to arms and brain,
and prayer
that that bulbed fruit
never be stained by sin,
that potency of truth

retain such peace,
and luminous grace
as now is felt within.
A grape on stem,
my child, this poem,
you, I, and the globed world,
growing and glowing
candescent at rim and center,
holding, held by, heaven.
Grape,
world,
man
poem,
God
on one cord.

## *Katherine Thayer Hobson*

### BEYOND DIMENSION

As one steps from worn sandals I leave the day,
And know that the rest of the night is mine,
Before I go back, as return I may
To abysmal Time.
Riding my dreams down creation's track,
Mouse hole and galaxy wheel through space –
What is minute or sublime?
Free of dimension, gravity, place
Sometimes I think I have seen God's back,
But never His face.

## *Barbara D. Holender*

### A GEODETIC VIEW

–No comment–said the president
of the Flat Earth Society,
confronted by earth's curvature
as photographed from outer space.
(Note that he did not recant.)

–The fact is–they told him . . .
No facts, please,
we all have facts. What people want
are meaningful measurements, such as
up is good and down is bad
and left is wrong. That's what a man
gauges his life by. Earth's all edges,
precipices, crevices,
and we have fears of falling.

Sometimes in nightmares I inhabit
a ball hung whirling in a void.
I cling like down on a dandelion,
knowing that one good puff . . ! and watch
everyone trying to get off.

Or worse, I wake in fear the world's
the shape we act as if it were:
a box within a box within
a box within, all opening in.

"Fact" is a chosen image from
the angle of your preference.
Near ground, where I fix my lens,
Round does not photograph. Round is

the verb "to know" intensified;
Round is Now, caught like a breath
till your ears pop and your eyes swim
and a long exhalation turns
earth over into time.

## *Glenna Holloway*

### THE INTERLOPERS

Beneath inverted black fir jungle
of water hyacinth roots underweaving my hidden bayou,
my diver's lamp the only hold with my world, I
disturb a concert of stripes: hundreds of
inch-long tetras silver-slanting right or left
as my hand directs. A king-size mud cat like
Genghis Khan eyes me from the olive drab floor.
And overhead! My secret boat!—impounded
since last summer—clamped listing in a wet/dry
vise, sun-half of bulbous green vases feigning
innocence with flowers. Night-half of fringe and
garland-chain, propeller upholstered in velvet.
I rip away the slimy grip and feel
hairy stalactites grow closer, determined
as topside kudzu. The gasoline-fed screw might
thresh one yard before losing. A new spring army
of trees wades out to make a stockade. Roman-helmeted
herons patrol the spreading perimeter above. Here,
the mighty Khan shares guard only with turtles. And I,
slave to light and lungs must fight myself free.

## *Frances Minturn Howard*

### STONES

Things grow on stones, though stones don't grow on
things—
Moss, lichen, weeds—all waverers in air.
Wind blows not through them but around them. Seas
Are parted and make monuments above them
Of surging white. The weightedness of stone
Belittles all that moves.

From what harsh melon were these earth-seeds split
That hug the hills,
Resist the bite of seas,
And on the bottom of the ocean squat?
Their dark tenacious passion
Is to endure.

Each stone
Is a small citadel
Against assaulting wind,
Recurrent sea,
The pull and heave and yaw of mortal transience,
That blows all bright and starry dust away.

Observe, beneath the moving water-sky
Green cities tower and blow,
Lengthen and grow,
With random currents move; but are not lost
Because, to green intransigence,
The rooted stone gives permanence.

There's no alloy in stone—
No transmutation in its character,

Like metal's cells that dance to cold, to heat;
Ground into smallest particles, it shows
No alteration in what makes it stone;
A grain of sand has mountains in its breast.

There are no absolutes—
Yet something must pretend
To be an absolute.
Not logic, nor a city, springs from air.
Without some ultimate hardness taken on trust
Nothing can build.

## *Dorothy Hughes*

### THE EXAM

When it was time, the teacher rolled up the screen,
and under it, encrusted on the black-board like a
 script of whipped cream
(Happy Birthday—) was the exam. The teacher walked
off like a queen and left us with the smell of chalk.

From the school, I could see Columbia campus, where
 the sun
lay simmering, and the brick walk stumbled through.
 And that wonder,
the observatory, with the peep in its roof like a
 slice of pie.
I could see the acropolis of upper campus, beyond reality.

I knew the answers. Blinded by the primary colors
of thirteen, I used learning like a sword, without
 love,

ignoring the enormous roar, the popular rule,
that you may excel in basket-ball, but not in school.

When the exam was almost over, the teacher came back,
drifting silently up and down the aisles. And there
 was that
in the myth of her, a fastness of years, that stirred
 in me
something neither primary nor pragmatic, but a
 gentling, a defeat.

The papers were gathered up, and we tousled our
 way to the door.
The room stiffened, desks striking iron talons into
 the floor.
I looked back and saw afternoon castling the campus
 wall,
windows smitten, and the observatory clasped in a
 fiery circle.

## *Colette Inez*

### INSTRUCTIONS FOR THE ERECTION OF A STATUE OF MYSELF IN CENTRAL PARK

Let me be formed with stone;
A slab of diorite between my ears
will do for brains,
a round cut ruby for a heart.

Breasts? Alabaster mounds
that will not sag from suckling time,
against which birds will bat their wings

and rain will stroke and wind . . .

Cold to sex, and blood and birth,
drape my marble thighs with snow.
Then let the lovers, hot with quarreling and tears,
stand in my shadow and kiss.

## *Jeremy Ingalls*

### POLITICAL SCIENCE

Alexander,
In a hurry for peace and therefore
Avid for empire,
Slashed the Gordian knot.
Misappraised, each Alexander
Is still called clever.

To mention
That a slashed knot is not undone
Is to be assured a bad press.
With every era, nonetheless,
The knot, slashed, knots itself again
Harder.

# *Florence B. Jacobs*

## WINDFALL

This was as promising as any bud
among the new leaves, after petals fell
in a June snowdrift, and the hard green fruit
began to swell;

Began to ripen under languid heat
and heavy dews, curved into perfect shape,
straining the sunshine through a skin that turned
dark as a grape.

Resisting with the stoutness of its hold
the livid thunderstorm, the August hail;
then loosened, crashing earthward in a wild
September gale;

Still lovely where it lies among the grass,
wine-dark and round, still snowy-fleshed and tart,
but not worth storing, for the cancerous bruise
deep in the heart. . . .

# *Grover Jacoby*

## DILEMMA IN CALIFORNIA

You are looking
Into a confusion of seasons and cultures;
Stains of orange and yellow dryness linger
Here and there among twigs almost winter-clean;

Now the date palm's jungle-splash of frond
Utters quite a summer accent.
Then a bird's voice,
One of spring's love trinkets,
Is picked up by the ear
And tossed among the scene's eclectic pleasures.

You leave the natural world by car
And after having parked,
Wander among neoclassic banks and office buildings,
Wondering whether to learn Nahuatl,
Or with these stale pilasters
Recognize the humanistic premise
Of Greek and Latin above everything–
Or take up Japanese.
(Far from this shelf of land
The islands stare,
And behind the islands, China,
A world of worlds and ages.)
Or go on with French and German,
And sip the filtered good of Europe
In Rilke, Verlaine, and the rest–
Or Spanish
Since Charles the Fifth once ruled the naked aborigines.

One foolish friend thinks it best to talk with London
By transcontinental, transatlantic telephone–
With Mr. Eliot of the gestured cadence,
To be advised of the most elegant futility.

Oh, well, forget it!
Shake off philosophies of heritage.
Snatch what you like from culture's great buffet.
Decisions are not made within the head
But through the lungs.

The air so winter-winterless,
This diamond atmosphere
Though flawed by intromission of phenomena,
Inhale it well.
Renovate perception,
Breathe, enjoy.

## *Marie B. Jaffe*

### BIRTHDAY CARD TO MYSELF

Some people at 58, start winning diplomas –
Others go into comas;
Me, I'm for the middle road –
I'm just happy to toss off an ode.
Even a sonnet or triolet
Give me a glow, rosy and violet.

Some people at 58, think it's late,
Start retiring;
Me, new zest I'm acquiring –
Morning, noon and night, I yearn to write.
So once in a while, I have style.
Sometimes the stuff is amusing;
But mostly it's pretty confusing.

Some people at 58, refuse all neighborly offers –
They're busy filling their coffers;
So occupied counting their money,
They are anti-social and funny.
Me, I'm a vulture when it comes to culture –
I can't get enough of it.
I dote on it.

Some people at 58, decide to take it easy –
About activities they feel queasy.
Me, I'm just getting my second wind –
I'm Pavlova; I'm Jenny Lind –
I'm anything but through –
I'm telling you.

Some people at 58, go into hibernation –
Their own shadows fill them with consternation.
Me, I'm just getting started –
Dance-footed, joy-hearted –
I feel great, at 58.

Some people at 58, refuse invitations,
Answer no phone calls,
Prepare to hide under moth-balls.
Me, I feel in the first blush of youth –
You insist on the truth? Uncivil! Uncouth!

Some people at 58, say their powers diminish –
So they call it their finish.
Me, I'm just getting hep – I'm in step –
I'm in the groove – I'm on the move –
I'm keen, I'm nifty –
I'm 8 and 50!

## *Oliver Jenkins*

### LEAVE-TAKING

What of tomorrow's weather,
What temper the sea and sky,
The wind in the heather?

We walk along the bluff
Through blowing grass and sand.
Year coming to an end.

Now the swift days are gone.
The year is going down
With the wind and sun . . . .

A last glance at the glass
And the crumpled almanac,
Then turn and not look back.

## *Ann Jonas*

### IN MEMORIAM: THEODORE ROETHKE

Now you are rooted in dark time
and give it form.
Your branches sing the night,
yet shimmer longer
than distances of birds.
You move in the color of winds.
The earth you molded in your hands
and nurtured into words,
shaping all seasons,
holds you in its poem.

## *Barbara Leslie Jordan*

### DUTCH ELM DISEASE

Lightning is swift to end a tree's green life
And wind can topple it within an hour,
Flame can consume it with a sudden rush,
Cold can destroy it with a glacial power.

But this slow, tortured ending should not come
While leaves still wave against a summer sky,
This creeping rot within the stalwart trunk
Which, inch by inch, will force the tree to die.

I must protest this unseen, evil thing
Which I am powerless to halt or cure.
For tree and man, alike, and for man's love,
Death should be quick and merciful and sure.

## *Hans Juergensen*

### TO MY DAUGHTER

This was her night, her winter
Quilted in the thinning snows
Of her already March thoughts;
Her wings about to fling her
Into red suns.

The old love moulted, rusting
On white dune – primavera roots
In her eyes, seeded to pierce

The frozen flesh of solitude,
Awaiting opened rivers.

She joins dream limbs to
Earth's torso, and they reach
Out their burgeoning cells –
Blood-fresh, flawless – like
Fluid steel: a resurrection.

Now let her comprehend star oceans
In the becoming of her own.

## *Hannah Kahn*

### WITHOUT COMPASS

It is as though I lived in time
that rises up in waves
while I attempt to hold the tide
with long white silken gloves

as though I, deafened by a sound,
spoke yet could not hear
my own voice nor the warning bell
that stammered in the air.

# *Douglas V. Kane*

## EVENING IN KYOTO

Samurai and swords
In shambles of the Shogun
Wax neuter to me,
As I rest in my hot bath
Dreaming of seasons:

Cherry-foam of April,
And bewitched chrysanthemums
Under the pearl moon,
And the long trek up *Fuji-san*
To a brow of snow . . . .

Hacking and haggling
In commerce, and the thick curse
Of streets, have now flown
The night's agenda. I rise
A red-bodied man.

A geisha drapes me
In silk, and I watch my scroll,
With branch and flower,
From a low board, saki-cupped,
With fries from the sea.

She strokes samisen
Or koto, blowing light pearls
From her lips in song,
And old poems vapor-brushed
By Hitomaro.

With happy Buddhas
We cast our lot. Paradise
Is a laughing moon
With a quiet motion toward
The *torii* of sleep.

## *Milton Kaplan*

### POETRY READING

Outside in the light of the neon sun
Five little girls are skipping rope
    *Down the Mississippi*
    *Where the green grass grows*
Up and down the glance they dance
    *Down the Mississippi*
Skirts flaring and collapsing
As the rope whips the pavement
Into breathing like a clock
    *Where the boats go push*
While the soapbubble vowels float upward
And break against the brick wall
Of the lecture hall inside which
    *Down the Mississippi*
    *Where the green grass grows*

O, says the poet, the toy
Balloon of his outcry wrinkling around
His breath as he starts to read
In the quiet room where people listen.

## *George Keithley*

### CHARLIE CHAPLIN HAS THE LAST LAUGH

The scene suggests a city full of schemes.
The Tramp taps his cane tip-pat tip-pat
and lolls by a lamppost looking at his shoes.
His pants are a bag of dreams.

His landlord flaps his fat chins on his collar,
strutting down the street like a side of beef.
He wears a bulge of banknotes in his hips
and a smile like the crease in a fresh dollar.

A smile that drips with malice when he trips over
someone's cane
and gathers himself in a gutter
where the rainwater runs in a river

and the Tramp stares at his feet feeling shy
at such success.
Left with his thumbing luck
he buttons his ravelled vest to his fly.

He limps by like a man bent with bundles.
His black breast curves like a crow's,
but his wax white eyes
flicker flicker as innocent as candles.

## *Martha Keller*

### SEA OF DUST

By the hands, by the sands of decay,
I am lapped and enwrapped and enwound.
The ship of the dead is a mound.
My shroud is the clay that I wear.
In a boat without oar, without sail,
I embark on the tide of despair,
On a waste without break, without bound,
Without wave, without wake, without shore.
By the dust in my throat and my hair,
By the sound of the dark I am drowned,
By the sigh of the dark, by its sound.
For no water nor wave is as loud,
However it whisper or wail,
As the rush and the deafening roar
Of the hush of the grave of the ground.

## *Mary Kennedy*

### RIDE INTO MORNING

It is my young mother driving along
the sandy roads of my childhood,
and there am I, a child of four,
sitting proudly beside a lovely lady.
On the way, on the way, on the way somewhere!
Swiftly moving into a beckoning unknown.
The horse is called Barney
after a friend of my father's.

A happy neigh as he answers the reins urging,
the light whip crackling in air
with high stepping, proud prancing,
brown haunches rocking, tail swishing
over the buckboard. His hooves
leave round marks in the damp white sand.
The wheels of the buggy splash as we ford
the leaf-brown waters of a shallow creek.
Morning coolness touches my face.
The air is sharp with pine.
A small tortoise in the road:
My mother reins in old Barney
and waits for it to cross. . . . a round,
dark object with thrusting eager head.
In its own time. In its own time.
I lean my cheek against the white muslin
of her sleeve. Contentedly I sense
that I, too, shall not be hurried.

Mother turn! Look deeply into my eyes,
reveal yourself. When I am an old woman
I shall long to understand, to know you
as you are now. To be sure that you know
of the love spilling over, as I sit trustfully
beside you, riding into the silver morning.
I hear the hoof beats, as my mother and I
and the times we lived in,
go softly thudding into oblivion.

## *Kenton Kilmer*

### THE LIVING POET
(John Louis Bonn, S. J.)

While the great wings are buoyed on eager air,
    See now, see now, how beautiful they are!
The piercing downward dart, or, upward, there,
The buffeting surge and rise, the eagle stare
    Down cloudy canyons to the ribboned fields.

With eagle's eye, with ringing, singing tongue,
    This is no bird to wait death for his song.
The towers of cloud with bells of song are hung.
On all the winds of earth the song is flung.
    The hills and forests hear it and are still.

Now wreathy clouds are stirred with beating wings,
    The vaulted sky will ring when he is gone
With tumult and the broken echoings,
Through hollow silence, of what now he sings.
    When the great wings are still, the gold eyes dim,
    His cloudy mountains will remember him.

## *James H. Koch*

### A DIALOGUE OF BONES

She: What's that?

He: A drum of thunder.

She: Another?

He: No, a silence now. Earth wakes to drink
Some more of Sun; and Spring has Winter riled.

She: I'd hoped for sounds of promises fulfilled.

He: What guarantees there were have long run out,
My dear; we've sounded our retreat toward dust.
Of me remains a rib, of you a skull
Whose cheek I feel as sharp and chill as steel.

She: I loved you warmly then, for when we kissed
Your cold nose tickled as it traced my length.

He: The rain's begun; this final rib will go.

She: I used to fear being left alone, but now . . .

He: You lost me piecemeal to the roots and rain
While this thistle grew where love had lain.

## *Linda Krenis*

### SONG FOR HER SLEEP

sing lullaby Ophelia child
with all your pretty wreaths of grief
and leaves like tears
that trail your face in long green vines

sing lullaby and wind your losses
in your hair Ophelia

fair your flowers are stones
that weigh you down

sing lullaby see how your gown
soaks up the stream
that hold you here
Ophelia floating unconsoled

## *Fania Kruger*

### THE TENTH JEW

The cold was bitter and the sky was red,
Within the Polish ghetto lay the dead.
And in one corner of a blasted wood
In wounded bleeding circle, nine men stood
Praying for the dead. When shadows draped
The fields with gray, these hunted had escaped—
Nine only out of hundreds burned and slain,
To offer *Kaddish,* grief's austere refrain.
No other left in a ghetto of red slaughter,
To join in prayer for absent son or daughter,
For mother, wife, all vanished in that day—
No tenth man for a *minyan* and to pray.

And though the Temple's law required that ten
Male voices must make valid grief's amen,
Shivering, moaning there, while bare boughs swayed,
Deep in the forest, only nine men prayed:
"*Yisgadal . . .*" Their quivering, plaintive chant
Rose hoarsely as they held their covenant—
Clothed in gray mist, a cowl of twilight haze,
Their faces pale as a frozen meadow glaze,

Nine voices growing faint and fainter. . . . Then
Suddenly from the gloom a sound—"Amen!"
A tenth voice, a *minyan!* They all turn to see:
Behold upon a starkly twisted tree
A tortured sufferer, murdered now anew.
Crucified Jesus, the tenth praying Jew.

## *Mabel M. Kuykendall*

### THE PENITENTE

His was a love not confined to the body;
and his was a sorrow as great as the cross
he bore up the mountain this year for atonement,
planting it firmly on the crown of the pass.

Yesterday he looked an age on his homestead;
with prayerful fingers he touched his young son;
his wife he held close in his arms and caressed her,
then rose from his seeding with an ache to be gone.

Exalted and silent he met other figures
to march in a column of shadow and pain.
He heard the flute wail as he reached the morada;
his heart embraced arctic and his mind fell prone
on the plowshare of Abel and the dagger of Cain.

On his knees, groveling, or erect in his trauma,
the master of punishment, himself, wept and tore
his flesh with the whips the desert had fashioned
to spatter his blood on the walls and the floor.

Beautiful rivers of blood grooved him warmly
and leaped in small flecks to the congregate stain;

but he barely heard the flute's flagellation
or his brothers' torment—his companions in tone.

"Do not twist southward," he said to his body;
"Do not bleed inward," he said to his soul;
and outside he shouldered the cross far too heavy
for three men, and dragged it up Calvary Trail.

Tomorrow his wife will stand trembling and staring
at leather reflecting the east turning red:
his shoes on his doorstep will be the announcement
of no more homecomings from processions of blood.
And no one will tell where he lies in the mountains,
consigned to the dust and the mercies of God.

Tomorrow his son will be dark in his thinking
as he lays the shoes gently at Our Lady's feet.
He will think of the long years before he can wear them
to join Father Jesus and the Brothers of Light.

## *Joan LaBombard*

### IN THE LION'S MONTH

Our lady of the fields,
Whose horn of plenty pours
Wild clover, quince and berry
And honey for the yield,
Your lord's in the ascendant,
And his ambassadors.

Lady, we praise your lord
Who sets small suns upon

Bough and field and meadow.
They are the sun's shadow,
A sun-struck progeny
Out of the lion's month.

And the birds around you, lady,
Wake with their sweet choirs
Your prodigies of flowers,
Your poppies heaped, the wheat
In the hollow of your hand,
And all extravagance

Of bough, bush and petal
Drowned in such pure light,
They shine like seraphim
Although that color's mortal,
But of your blinding sheaves,
The likest paradigm.

The innocent and the young
So make of your green myth
Epithalamiums,
They marry with the sun
And leave the sheaves unbound
To pay you courtesy.

O when the gold fanfare
Proclaims your lord's advent
And every blandishment
Of honey's on the tongue,
Lady, your fields are ripe
For every harvesting.

## *Norma Lay*

### SOUTH-NORTH ROAD, GOOD FRIDAY MORNING

Beside me, breakfasting at the HoTo counter,
a child has the face of a Ghirlandajo
angel.

At gas pump, painter from my car-top boat
tangles.
Tall individual of the dark-music race
with jackknife, know-how offers to untie,
tie.

Does.

NOT TRUE THAT GOD IS NOT.

I hang my starched white sailor jacket
window-side-out, in Easter
certainty.

## *Laura Laurene Le Gear*

### EARTH RUNNER

The heart runs barefoot through cool tallow trees
With feet more nimble than a swift killdee's,
Where grasses swish quick silver up the knees.

Through eager urchin hours, past years that dwarf,
Alone, it skips blue clovered, sea-less wharf,

And wears each ribboned rainbow for a scarf;

Naked in thought, when skies glow salmon-finned,
While young flowers wander woods, moss-moccasined.
One born twin sister to our orphaned wind.

Fathered by cloud, half-mothered by frail moon,
Lonely as bittern or mad marsh's loon . . .
The barefoot heart runs headlong through its June.

## *Cornel Lengyel*

### NOON SONG

(1)
Noon so clear
        night so long:
Shan't I dare
        invent a song?

(2)
Time so little
        change so near:
Words so brittle
        who will hear?

(3)
Yet let who can
        turn breath to song:
Love in man
        lasts not long.

# *Florence Becker Lennon*

## COEXISTENCE

Dear St. Francis,
What must I do about raccoons?
The neighbors seem to give them a bad name:
They gang up on our dogs and cats to kill
They scoop the goldfish from the lily pool
They scratch and even bite the human hand
They carry rabies.
It may be so.

They wear a question on their faces
They never foul their feeding places
They bring such gaiety to my patio
They have such fluffy babies.
They troop in like a robber band
Play Harlequin and Columbine and Fool—
Hang from the vine, peer in the window, mill,
Scuffle, importune, pray—who wants them tame?
Please, may I feed the naughty Pantaloons,
Dear St. Francis?

# *D. J. Lepore*

## FOOTNOTE TO MAN

Now this country, this parable of stone,
Steel and wood horizontal to the bone
Whitened and heaped beyond all horizons,
Timelessly wheels without compass, sextant
For all, and all the sage inhabitants.

O Country desolate, Time once knew thee
Fair. Now thou art stripped of all identity.
If thou hadst only known the things for peace!
Summon not the nightingale nor the wren,
For worms move silently through silent men.

## *Adele Levi*

### SOUND OF SEA

O this world, this wheel
water vane of light in the lowered green dawn:
green upon the morning, the hills
rising around corners
and left-lying sound of sea.

How many have skin for light to pour through
or eyes for tree trunks to measure,
eyes like hand mirrors
seeing backward and forward—sky?

We walk through doors and disappear
into the grain-grind of rooms,
and now the uplands, the hill corners
wave a sound and texture of sea.

## *Elias Lieberman*

### BALLADE OF THE HERACLITAN FLUX

Hubris and pomp in the waning light
Of palace lamps must disappear:
Thebes is a column in Karnak's blight,
Babylon echoes a prophet's jeer,
The Wailing Wall is an undried tear
And a hymn to the past is the Parthenon.
Dim are some beacons which once shone clear
As the stream of change flows on and on.

Midge of a tremulous summer night
Gods of the fabulous yesteryear,
You came and went like a swallow's flight
When autumn and chilling winds draw near;
Time tolls a bell at an ornate bier
And kings drift away to oblivion,
Feathers of chance in winds that veer
As the stream of change flows on and on.

Cardinal throned or acolyte,
Marcher ahead or straggler in rear,
Lance-proud left or thrust-proof right,
Permanence ever evades our sphere.
Ruin hides where the victors cheer,
Victory bides where the vanquished run;
Fame is a garland turning sere
As the stream of change flows on and on.

*Envoy*

Fashions hint at a hidden fear;
Modernity shifts at a dip of the sun,
Lingering only a moment here
As the stream of change flows on and on.

## *Marion Lineaweaver*

### THINGS THAT WERE STILL ALIVE

After your funeral I went back to the house alone.
I could not close my eyes; they were stretched with horror.
I packed your clothes out of sight, your smaller belongings,
Your photograph, even, and then I lay down in my black
 dress.
I could not undo the zipper.

That night our cat came in from her hunting
And crouched beside me, not on your side of the bed,
Not purring. When dawn struck blood-red at the windows
She had to be fed. . . . I remembered other things
That were still alive and went out back
To water the pea patch, the peppers, cucumbers,
Lettuce, corn, and the reliable
Pink moss roses you had put in for me.

I pulled a radish, bit into its earthy crispness.
All day I carried its tuft of leaves in my fist
Walking where you had walked, telling myself
That plants could in some way prove immortality.
I shall have to look into that
By keeping the garden up, caring for what you planned.

## *Carolyn Wilson Link*

### THE POEM IS

To know the quickening, the pain
and, though it need the surgeon's knife,

release the creature from the brain
to eloquent and separate life,
its lineage as plain to see
as when a small and serrate leaf
describes, root, bole, and flower, the tree,
or one tear globes the whole of grief.

## *Gordden Link*

### POETRY AND PHYSICS

There is minuscule pause
at the junction of four dimensions
when the poem suspends itself in time and space
with abstract edges touching no ganglion's end
or thing or shadow of thinking.

At this infinitesimal delay
in the torrents of time
and the cataracts of curving space
that mate to spawn infinity,
the poem is ignorant of self or form
or destiny or pulse or sound.

It might emerge heroic
from this fractional log jam of history
as sermon or music or design or dream,
and only God who owes His being
Himself to this intricate phenomenon
can know how many poems
stipple our past disguised as symphonies
or steeples or religious revivals
or the staring skulls of dream upon the sands

that bury half-remembered races.

And this is well: if a poem survived
from every impulse man has had
to fossilize himself in song,
our heritage from history would be
mounds of memorial star-high and eternity-wide;
the topheavy world would stagger through the dark
uninhabited and cold and doomed
to never ending unawareness of man's capacity
for constructing nonconformist deities,
for translating tribal rhythms into a way of life,
for splitting hairs and infinitives and atoms.

## *Virginia Linton*

### CLOSE BY THE MANGROVE MEADOWS

From such a shore a man can throw a fish
Into the air, and bring a bird down from
The sky, or, just as likely, half a hundred—
Gulls and terns, slipping their wings through aisles
Of air which bear the lift of long, sea-swells;
Or, he can pull a fish up from the sea
With fins like the wings of a bird.

From such a shore in a blue calm, the sea
Comes up to meet the sky with no horizon
Which the eye can find—while the heron stands,
Leaning from his spit of sand, and stares into
The water of the cove, where the sea-floor
Shows, at noon, the coral hills rolling beneath
The slow drift of a floating moon;

And when a man casts out a line, it unwinds
Toward the flat reach of the sea, whipping thin
Sound from silence as it flies, and drops
Upon the surface of the water, or, just
As likely, on the bottom of the sky—
While sea-birds cry high as they dive, and fish
Leap to divide with stiffened fins, shallows
Shining where the air begins.

## *Robert Lloyd*

### NIGHTFALL IN THE JEMEZ MOUNTAINS ABOVE THE VALLE GRANDE

these pines
stand for it
*calligraphy*
stand to be stood among
to return to it
standing
a script of forms
upon the land
moving against skyscape
as i move across the earth
the pines
scribing both the rooted
and the animal view
against cloud
the volcano rim
and across
the palimpsests of air and light
and the eye

and evening clear
the meadows
close
as the sky uncolors
days-eyes in clearing
underfoot
and stars in clearings
overhead
obscured by clouds
only the brushstrokes
of these pines stand
over this closed circle
now without horizon
the evening cleared
to the closing black
and my eyes dilate
to tracelight
before the reflex
narrowing at the human
circle of a single lanternlight
beamed square
from the cabin windows
circled
at my walk home
these encircling pines
now must be strode to
to be found and touched
until morning
then
into lanternlight and sleep
only these pines brush
blackness
only the eyes can read
καλλιδραφια
in beauty it is written
blackness

only the eyes wrote
where

## *Edith Lodge*

### TEMPO OF SEASON

The crickets, merry metronomes, that tick
Warm hours away until allegro summer
Goes too soon, then slow to largo tempo,
As autumn, in grave pavane, moves to winter,
Retardando, when tiny clocks run down
And the year comes to rest, leaving only
Silence, crystal still, in a frosty night.

## *Louise Louis*

### THE TREE

As he looked back
he saw a tree. It touched
a star some nights; other times
it stood like him, dripping with dark.

He must have slept with it
a thousand times. An Arabian Night's
capacity it had for being
different and the same . . .

Once, he dreamed he melted

into it. Drove its leaves as shepherd
with a flock. The tree took names
for seasons . . . After the funeral

it filled a vacuum. The need to buy
to own or to dispossess . . . Something
about the years brought back
the tree. The time they counted
in his hearing rings that told
how old it was when they improved
the highway by taking it
down . . .

except it made translation
and negotiates as ever
in his head . . . . so when he stands
in torment of the modern conquests
and his measurements inadequate
to touch a star . . . . he has sanctuary
where the Tree is.

## *Ted Lovington Jr.*

### THE DEATH OF ROMAN NOSE

On Beecher's Island in '68
The Spencer rifles roared
At the waves of bright Cheyenne,
The Arapho and Brule Sioux.

The ragged troopers fought
From the hungry spit of sand,
Fired from the rear of horses

Arrow-stung and fallen,
And fired from shallow pits.

They broke the Cheyenne wave
And shattered the Arapho
And scattering of Brule Sioux
Until at last, at last alone,

Shaking his sticklike rifle
In the bullet-brittle air
Rode the mighty Roman Nose,
Yellow painted on his horse,
Proud and eagle-feather plumed.

Alone, riding at Beecher's Island,
A rage of bullets stung him,
Flung him from the horse,
Shattered his valiancy at last
In the sand-roiled waters
Beneath the sun's colossal chant.

## *Gertrude May Lutz*

### BIP AND THE BUTTERFLY
*for Marcel Marceau*

You, Bip, clown with painted white face,
flower trembling atop your battered high hat,
your trouser legs lift lightly, deftly,
through byways of meadow . . . the flitting
butterfly just out of reach.

Then the catch!

In forlorn hands, mime of wings is still.
A black curtain frames your sorrow;
your tears sting in our eyes . . .

Suddenly long fingers spread wide,
joy curves upward your wide astonished mouth—
your eyes are rounds of delight!

In mind's eye, we watch the bright creature
stir, slowly lift, flutter to air . . .
watch your curious flower moving
with elegance and grace atop your hat's
jubilant crown, following flight
of lifting life . . . and you . . . off stage . . .

Bip, clown with painted white face—
how you do mix eloquence with no spoken word!

## *Gloria MacArthur*

### DIARY OF AN UNKNOWN

When Charlie Massey went to war,
he bragged on what he'd left behind
—a horse, a wagon, and a whore.
Somehow, they intertwined
the way he told it. One was sorry
—sorrier than Satan. Feeble.
Ash—one—of a hot glory.
Babel, one was. Trouble
nobly borne. But which or who
was what? You reckon Charlie knew?
Like spores that dumb darkness drew
its breath, until the smut of war

was more unreal than Massey's whore.
And it didn't matter any more.

## *Marion M. Madsen*

### FRAGMENT

All things come to a standstill here in the grass.
Here in the tall grass, even the wind is stopped
And the sun is caught in the topmost branch of the cedar;
Higher a hawk repeats his lazy loop, never alighting.

And should we leave, nothing at all would be changed
But the world would pick up its old routine
Where it left off this morning.

O hold me, hold me now while clocks are defeated,
While the chimes and bells that toll the passing hour
Are tangled here in the tall grass under our fingers.

This is a fragment cut from the stone of the ages;
Do not lose it, while the world waits
Holding its monumental breath here in the tall grass.

## *Francis Maguire*

### TO A DOG BARKING AT NIGHT

I know, baby: as you fear,
barking brings no one back.
But it's a noise in an empty world
and it helps to fill the dark.

## *Margery Mansfield*

### MARRIAGE SONG

And if you want to and do
Ask something more of love
Than a saying, "I am through
And off and down the road,
Where other loves gleam new,"
Then come and take this load.

But do not ask me why
Love ripens into care,
And is no more a cry
Of joy and swift despair.
That soft young dove must die,
Or love will not stay there.

No thanks will be returned
For speaking of such things,
But be not too concerned
If your heart no longer sings.
Something of birds I learned
By looking at their wings.

## *Adrianne Marcus*

### PROVISIONS OF LATITUDE

1. The Whales

I crouch on the high granite
Watching the grey processional

Advance on the northern waters.
In the slanted light, their fine spray
Gleams like delicate fountains,
And their bellies, white as salt,
Curve to the first icy current
Off Alaska. Old whales, sounding,
Test the blackness, or leap
Into the air, gleaming silver
As if harpoons still lay siege
To their fierce and mottled backs.
They talk among themselves:
Mouths like canyons, deep and riveted,
Feasting on tides of fish as they move
Steady across the pull of an ocean,
Heaving and huge as their element.
Only a man swept into that roaring tomb,
Beholding himself in darkness like creation,
Hearing the waters churn and rush
Through the prison jaws, feels
The limits of his size,
The uselessness of hands. Locked
In this stench of rotting fish
And seaweed for three days, then spewed
Out on a blinding shore,
His eyes crusted with salt and darkness,
Fearing the light almost as much
As the black smell of that whale.

2. Born in Pisces

Three castles built, the wide moat
Fills with water, the intricate towers dissolve.
Suddenly, the wind shifts over the thin horizon,
The tide turns south, stippled with whitecaps.
As I walk the changing beach, finding a few agates,
Holding them into the light to see

The pure cut of the ocean, divisions of stone,
I watch the narrow inlet for the first sign
Of a heavy keel clocking the grey water.

I live by a season of tides,
Hearing the ocean sing like a lover,
The moon pulling the water
As it rises and thrusts.
August, the ocean tears
At the barren rocks, splintering
The torn boats of the fishermen;
And beyond the thickening point,
The fog hangs in one vast tower.

Each day, scouring the beach for driftwood,
blunt stones, shells without purpose,
I gather wood for a fire, remnants of a small vessel.
Gathering the sticks layer by layer,
I pray for deliverance,
For the drowned sailors, their nets
Still brimming with fish, and for myself,
As their wife and mother.

## *Karen Marmon*

### TIDEPOOLS

At the surf's edge,
catching tossed up shells
fast from the foam
before they slip back—
loving you's like that.

I stir in the depths,
hide with the crabs in the kelp.
Barnacles clumped on a shell
suck air.
Doubt chills the sea.

Yet the same tide sometimes
catches us both
at the place
where the wave breaks.

## *Lenore G. Marshall*

### DREAM

At this waystation the ship goes through the narrows.
I have been here before. It is night.
An anchored barge appears or call it an island dock
Or bar like customs, alone forever. We edge against it,
Last stop before open sea.
Our ship must pass between locks.
I thought I would never see Far-land again. This is the
  last time,
I said. It is never the last.

Or never leave home again. Yet the voyage begins again.
Sprung from the deep
That fate, flat on the water like a raft,
My island, my isolate, waits.
Then carrying lanterns, single as lighthouse men,
Lighthouse turned darkhouse, quiet turned quay, men
  turned shadow
In silence usher us through.

O never again will I come this way
I said, This way, never again.
No more! No more!
I thought: I have been here before.

## *Patricia Martin*

### WOULD YOU CARE TO LEAVE A MESSAGE?

*Yes.*
Tell them we waited with all the time we had
and, being vocal, phrased the thing we said
in every language, praying it be heard.

Tell them the word
to hold is Peace. Say that we studied war
and found it waste. (Repeat the message, please.)
Yes.

And if they do not even
recall our name; if they receive in anger
this counsel from a stranger; still their day
will hear a truth we tore our lungs to say.

## *Anne Marx*

### BLOOD STRANGERS

Alone in the teeming terminal
I am shoved like a loose canoe

and drift into streams near the newsstand,
as two young men hail me, converging.
Unaware of their family ties,
they commute from different directions;
introduced, part conventional lips
in smiles of fleeting engagement.

Without recognition, that meeting;
only vagueness of distant relations.
Second cousins, too far removed
for more than a casual greeting.
Same features, like cruising ships
assigned to opposite routes,
untouched by crossing and passing;
they ascend equal numbers of steps
on different sides of the station.

Their great-grandfather came from Munich,
became a great musician . . .
at ninety, died in Dachau.
(Can't they see? Don't they know?)
Both descended from him
the same number of bloody steps,
each by a different line.
But nothing could have meant less
to those two grey suits and dark ties.

Alone again, I recall him,
an ancestor tall and unbent . . .
no name of concern for intent
young men on their way to success.
And I hasten to buy my paper
to bury myself in the present
stifling pangs of the past—

all around me the hurry, the waste.

## *Madeline Mason*

### THE OAKLEAF
(Sonnet in a New Form)

As I would hunt for clover, one fourleaf
Somewhere concealed among the crowding grass,
And push the blades aside that all spring back
Against my hands and eyes, my wild belief
In luck still findable, so I'd unmass
All these not you, their samenesses unstack
To see, unique, your gold against their black.
I shall not find, and if I did, you'd pass
As any stranger would, not mine to know.
Sun-grafted so, the image on mind's glass,
The everlasting glory of the brief.
I see again that sharp, once-only glow,
A woodland all unleafed, against its snow
The darkening gold of one wind-laid oakleaf.

## *Marcia Lee Masters*

### MY FATHER'S LAST JOURNEY

Upon his last journey
From east to west,
And to his childhood home,
Deep down in Illinois,
His casket came, at night.

Alone, unlighted,
It bumped into that endless depot

Where east meets west;
No stars; no lamps; no guards;
Only the mist,—

And then was transferred in the shapeless fog
Into another train. . . .

The fog upon those tracks;
The waiting train, more massive than a steer;
And all that darkness bearing down.

. . . . .

And I remember what my brother said:
"I led his casket to the other train,
Along deserted tracks;
I followed it as long as I could follow,

Then, I turned back."

## *Harry M. Meacham*

### TELEGRAPH WIRES

The road surrenders to the frowning hill
And crawls in lowly and circuitous ways,
But you, with Jovian stride and mighty will
Transcend the barriers of space and days.
As taut as strings on the Artemian bow,
And swift as her dread arrows, and as sharp,
Your simple messages of timeless woe
Go singing like some other-worldly harp.
Before the poet spells a tortured page,
Or reads its meaning from some ancient year

In long forgotten tongue of buried age,
You flash across the world, a smile, a tear.

Let others wear the muse's tragic mask,
No art can dare your solitary task.

## *Samuel Menashe*

### THE BARE TREE

These poems are in memory of my mother who once said to me, "When one sees the tree in leaf one thinks the beauty of the tree is in its leaves, and then one sees the bare tree."

1

Now dry stone holds
Your hopeful head
Your wise brown eyes
And precise nose

Your mouth is dead

2

The silence is vast
I am still and wander
Keeping you in mind
There is never enough
Time to know another

3

Root of my soul
Split the stone
Which holds you—
Be overthrown
Tomb I own

4

Darkness forged
Becomes a star
At whose core
You, dead, are

5

I will make you a landscape
Spread forth as waves run

## *Gladys Merrifield*

### PILGRIM

Now this aftermath
upward. The clearing path
at twilight is patched with old snow
that fell I know not when
so curtained then
the world I left, toward which again I go.

Only the dwindling scars of lethal drifts

dappling my pungent earth with scattered white
spell in thin fossil shapes lost worlds of time.

Now up ahead remembered sky, my night
flung bold again, erupts from locked horizons,
quickens these limbs, this mind: I move in wonder
as though unlocked but now from Adam's rib.

## *Gerard Previn Meyer*

### IN ANNE FRANK'S HOUSE

In Anne Frank's house we climbed the stair
the rickety stair that led nowhere
nowhere one would want to go

These steps you took, Anne Frank, into
a future that you never knew
unless that future time inherit
something of your timeless spirit . . .

Timeless? Ah, you had no time
from the moment you began your climb:
no time for childhood, youth, or age:
all time stopped then, like a page
turned down, to mark the place where we
might stop too. Eternity
alone was waiting, lurking there
in the rooms beyond the turn of the stair
in the windows on a painted world
where past and present and future curled
together in a tight cocoon . . .

One thinks: "It's bound to open soon,
and then bright wings will whisper out
what all that waiting was about . . ."

And then the creaking stair recalls
there came no breaking down of walls
to let in motion, air, and light:
only steps stamping up the flight
then, brutal jackboots kicking in
the door: then, where the door had been,
a gaping wound that bled into
a world that ever smaller grew
until there was no world . . .

And still
you raised, Anne Frank, against all ill
your voice that even now maintains
there is a hope escapes the chains
that mankind seeks to bind the soul with:
a hope that we can make us whole with . . .

IN ANNE FRANK'S HOUSE WE CLIMBED THE
STAIR
THE RICKETY STAIR THAT LED NOWHERE

## *Edward L. Meyerson*

### "THE FIXER"

(Based on Bernard Malamud's novel of the same name)

Did God in his petulance
Forsake him while
The flame flickered?

Skin is a fragile disguise
Of will that bends
But does not quickly break;

Or did it miraculously strengthen
Before his tormentors
Could shatter the shell?

Solitary, burrowed confinement
Did not keep away
Companions of the mind,

Though like fantasies forboding
They drifted into grotesque dreams
That dispelled the human image.

The jailer defiled his flesh,
Corroded his guts
While God brooded

And wavered in
The agnostic musing
Of the fixer.

Confess, confess
You will never again
Walk in the sunlight—

Instead, he kissed
The sudden beam of dawn
On the wall

And stripped the scrolls
For revelation, perchance
A covenant with God?

They poured his urine
Over the whitened shrunken head,
Disrobed him, awake or asleep,

For phantom weapons;
But unrevealed was the
Flaming sword of innocence

That one day, after God
Unforgiving, it would seem, had fled,
Suddenly severed his bondage;

Then like Lazarus, the fixer
Arose from the dead,
A colossus among the incredulous living.

## *Helene Mullins*

### TERZA RIMA

In the tall grasses the lion tracks his prey,
The blood of the zebra and the antelope
Spurts in the air through all their passion-play.

The python winds itself like a strangling rope
Around the tiger's body and in the cruel
Web of the spider the fly must blindly grope.

Incessantly the ancient and fierce renewal
Of war among different forms of life takes place.
No interlude in the immemorial duel.

The wolf devours the lamb and the cat gives chase

To the frantic mouse, the strong pursues the weak,
And death is the end of every desperate race.

Man is the only animal trained to seek
Destruction of its own kind: not yet can he
Envision rapport between powerful and meek.

Yet on this law of nature inexorably
Depends the survival of humanity.

## *William D. Mundell*

### PASTURE FOR OLD HORSES

From their stalls, gaunt after their long labors,
We led them out to their new pasture
In the somnolent hills—unharnessed
Except for the weightless feel of the tight leathers
Still in the burning of their flesh.
We let them drink at the cool trough,
And the water sang to their blood.
The morning smoldered in such stillness
Their ears hurt, hunting the harsh word
That we could not speak, and there fell
Funneled to their senses only the music.
They came with a loose rein in their excitement,
Only stopping, to gaze with wonder
At the fresh wound in the hill's side.
We removed their half-wanted and familiar bridles.
They stood pierced by the sudden strangeness.
Our kindness spoke in the quick ending,
Except the bending and the slow shovelling.
—And the wound of the hill will heal
Save for the rummaging of the red foxes.

## *Starr Nelson*

### THE MYTH IN THE VEIN

No Perseus rides this gale of splintered stone,
this dark wave swollen with rubble of centuries;
no Attic shapes are here,—the brain debrides
its house of myth as death debrides the bone.
Clotted with marble flinders, with sequins of gold gods,
is the dead sea that stains the Sphinx's knees;
the Swan, the Bull, swim gelded through the skies.

And yet, though never legend foam from them, nor song,
nor a name for a star, these are Andromeda's tears;
this is the dew on the rock, the long night long.

Is it only the blood too bright in the white wrist hears
the blue-steel-scaled, the saurian throat uprise,
hiss, shudder the granite surf to a clash of spears?
Only the Hellene iris wild in her eyes
as the coiled swerve, the slow ichthyotic scumble
through canyons cobalt with the dragon's breath,
topples the Ilian towers to timeless doom?

This skyscraper leans like a cliff; the four faces of the room
say nothing, their glass eyes close. Always her body trembles,
being bound. Only her blood, remembering how, once, tall,
Life split Death with a sword, lets the starless night fall.

## *Margaret Newlin*

### MARCH 17

Here's a tin button
Made in Japan.
'Kiss me', it says, 'I'm Irish.'
Dog knows I'm a moody sort.
These muddy days not yet warm
Get me down.

At my father's wake
Someone called my uncle 'Doctor'
Which made his day.
When he can pace a straight line
He floorwalks for men's clothing.
Nine of them, mind you,
Looking like Barrymores or kings.
The boys married workers,
Which was lucky, and my mother got my father.
Ennuied, except by mirror-talk,
She primped three quarter-centuries away.
But now our cabbage-rose grows vegetable
And will not even see a priest.

What am I to do
When they won't let her in their graveyard?
Dig up my father, pack the stone,
And migrate to some Jewish plot?
Lord knows we celts need wine or saints.
Our brand of beauty's not enough
Whether it queens in gems and fur
Or smoulders, nunlike, from white pages.

## *Louise Townsend Nicholl*

### OF WATER AND OF THIRST

Life is thirst and water for its slaking,
Water leaping from the source
To the surface watercourse.
Mothered not by making tide
Or the salty ocean bed,
Freshet, waterfall, and torrent,
Spate and cataract and current
Are with wellspring, fountainhead,
Deep in earth identified.

Life is water and the throat its mate,
Mystery of every taking.
Flesh and spirit, god and man,
Mortal penalty and plan,
He who gave the living water
Spake the dying word, "I thirst."

## *B. H. Oakes*

### OLD MAN ALONE

Does an old man think
alone in his bed . . . the
sheet a cover of iron
on wasted knees . . his
pillow a rectangle of
concrete? In this musty
room acrid with tobacco

and apples he tries to
memorize faces in faded
photos tucked around a
clouded mirror but they
are vague shapes marching
through his brain . . dragging
their heels on his forehead.
Fretful from thinking he
dozes intermittently but
his stentorian breathing
soon awakens him. Spraddle
legged and mumbling he plucks
the blanket his mind adrift.
It will take a while to remember
that he is marooned . . he must
lie quietly . . patiently. His
bed is an island.

## *Katherine O'Brien*

### EINSTEIN AND THE ICE-CREAM CONE

His first day at Princeton, the legend goes,
he went for a stroll (in his rumpled clothes).
He entered a coffee-shop—moment of doubt—
then climbed on a stool and looked about.
Beside him a frosh, likewise strange and alone,
consoling himself with an ice-cream cone.

Now Einstein's glee
was plain to see
at the sight of a cone with a sphere on top
(in the hand of a frosh in a sandwich shop)

and—O incredible—
completely edible!

He smiled at the frosh, then the waiter came,
and Einstein gestured he'd like the same,
and they sat there nibbling, suddenly kin,
with no common language to verbalize in,
but foreign no longer, no longer alone,
with the fellowship bond of an ice-cream cone.

## *Mary Oliver*

### HATTIE BLOOM

*She was,* Grandfather said, *a fly-by-night,*
*And did just what you'd guess her kind would do!*
Listening behind the door, I thought of Hattie
Who'd sailed the town trailing her silks like wings
And seemed to me as elegant and pale
As any night bird cruising in its feathers.
She'd made my uncle wild, that much I knew.
Though he was grown, he wept; though he was strong,
She taught him what it was to want and fail.

*True to her kind!* Grandfather said, and sneered.
*A fly-by-night! Come to your senses, boy!*
But it was months before my uncle turned
Back to the world, before his eyes grew mild;
And it was years before he loved again.
And what was I to think of such conclusions—
Pressed to the door, a small and curious child
Eavesdropping on the terrifying world
Of sons and fathers talking of their women?

I knew that Hattie Bloom had run away
The night before, gone like a gust of wind
On the night train, her perfumes like a veil
Left on the platform; and I knew somehow
The kind of life she lived—yet understood
That love, which made my gentle uncle wild,
Might also change a painted girl to gold.
The dream that smiled and trailed its silken wing
Was what my uncle grieved for; and I thought
The truth of love was that in truth, for him,
Lost Hattie Bloom became that perfect thing.

## *Jennie M. Palen*

### CORNFIELD WITH CROWS

Would you have hungered so for light, Vincent
(Van Gogh of whom the Van Goghs were then ashamed)
except for the grime and dark of that Belgian mine,
coal dust rooted in your every pore?
Would you have cried out so passionately for color
except for the drabness of the potato fields, existence
(the patina of bacon smoke and dirty unpeeled potatoes)
shared with diggers, sleep
(the poor man's wealth) denied you?
Later, from that blazing bedroom of your yellow house
at Arles,
would you have trudged against pain to the fierce wheat
fields
except for those scores of rough-sketched peasants
always working—always in motion
(learning, under failure's flagellation, what old masters
never had known)?

Now, at last, in your paintings,
wheat is a crashing sea of sun, and cypress trees leap up
like flame,
hills a tumultuous gesture.

The French say, "Bring up a raven and he will peck out
your eyes."
What had your furies done to you, Vincent,
when at Auvers you splattered canvas with that image of
fear
Cornfield with Crows?
Contorted sky, writhing corn, menacing birds—
was it for these you shot yourself that afternoon?
*But the crows were only burnt scraps, Vincent,*
*streeling on wind.*

## *Winthrop Palmer*

### WHEN THE WORD WAS GOD

Who are these people, wind – water –
the palm tree – the mangrove –
the order of birds?
The created, not made.

The wind hides in a cave
or rages in search of a victim.
Left to itself water is quiet enough;
a scamper, a ribbon under
the delicate feet of the heron.

A palm tree, that old accordian
player, addresses himself to the sky.

In a mangrove thicket, a choir —
    the sandpiper, the nuthatch, the
    black-bellied plover — twitter,
    tootle, whistle, chirrup, whee.

As for the pelican, mendicant friar,
    market basket under his chin,
    he collects at every pier.

## *Linda Pastan*

### WHITE

"I love white things. Oh, I love white." Andrew Wyeth

In the bright spectrum of years
white encompasses all colors:
the baby's milk days—
two breasts like hemispheres
of earth seen from far space;
the delight of sheets,
the final sheet
waiting to cover the blank face;
shells, bread, the moon over the cold lake;
a sky packed tight with snow
like crowds held by roped barriers
that finally break;
the mildness of flesh, the brutalities of bone,
and always, always the bare page demanding its poem.

## *Edmund Pennant*

### HUNGARIAN RAIN

Watertalk voices on my roof declaim
down the loud chute to iron lilacs
and murmer into the mute of whey
and caved-in snowbanks,

Magyar lingo from my mother's
homeland. I hear, I recognize
but do not understand.

Listen, she says, reaching my hand
under a melancholy cloud,
and teaches me by touch how dreams
go down the drain.

## *Grace Perry*

### DAHLIA

Like the dahlia
words break surface
and open out
upon a sea of green
then for a season
offer plates of colour
wavering in windruffled rows.
I walk among them
as they join and separate
nodding to one another

in discreet recognition
shaking feathery heads
in the stilted manner of suspended birds.
I listen and do not hear them.
Eyes closed
I wait for the surprise
of perfumed plumage—
there is none.
I touch.
No formal body moves
beneath the flower face.
The wheel of halfclosed petals
holds layers of silent tongues
locked at the centre
over the shaft sucking moist life
from the buried root.
The stem dries yellow
and the colours spill
upon the dark feet
of their origin.
Only the root knows
all the deaths we are made of
and that brown dwarf with folded skin
demands no meaning.
The root born old
swells under warm coverings
of earth and mouldering leaves.
There is no indecision
in the calm tunnelling into darkness
to accept and store
a memory of sunbright petals
in eternal cells
and build in secret
so that the present death of dahlias
implies no danger.

Next year
we shall not need
to search elsewhere
for flowers.

## *Frank Peters*

### TO ROBERT FROST

Father, I have brought you venison,
Excuse the delay, thrush music
Held me; on my way, I watched the sun
Fall down the west; the moon essay
With what sad steps
Upon her faithless spouse.

But, Father, tell me why
Point all these birches to the sky?
Why bouts the stranger
With these beechen blocks? Your locks
The winter occupy?
The furrows in your brow have gone to seed
And gullied all your acreage; no need
To worry now, – I will mend the wall.

Come, Father, eat; no scheming hand
Has spiced this sauce; the bow
Of your firstborn has tamed this fat.
Then bless me, Father, – prophesy;
Feel me; no supplanter am I.

# *Jenny Lind Porter*

## THE QUIET WINDOW

The quiet window where I stand
So quietly, looks on a land
My neighbors of habitual eyes
        Would hardly dare to recognize.

Upon the leafed and speaking tree
A troop of spirit company,
Rejuvenant and welcome band,
Is wise and bright on every hand,
And like an Ariel there flies
A soul forgetful of the ties
My neighbors of habitual eyes
Would gasp to see and recognize.

The quiet window greys and turns
To twilight, yet the vision burns,
And in the midnight hours free
It blazes like a noon in me.
Nothing is ever fixed or planned
For one who has divine command.
An urgency upon him lies
To save the world that hourly dies
For neighbors of habitual eyes
Someday to see and recognize.

## *Nancy Price*

### STAINED GLASS

From the day side you are pot-metal, no more
than crosshatch and stipple of dull planes,
propped by iron bars to the downpour
punishment of the rains.
You are old wounds, bits of bubble and streak,
scabbed crust of lichen and heat grooves,
cobwebs, soldering, leads that leak—
yet turn your face to me and the sun moves
by grace of your red scars; your blues lock
all heaven in place, a shelter. I forget
in such light how the mullions crack and pock,
how the north wind buckles the leads yet,
how your iron bleeds down the rock.

## *Elizabeth Randall-Mills*

### A CLOUD OF WITNESSES

No man is singular
But aureoled to "we",
Pitched to chorus in their
Felicity

Who are not silences,
Who flock the enlivened air,
Stripped of their absences,
Immensely here.

The coming of their love
Levels to earth their truth,
And polishes noon-bright
Our belief.

They are the ripeness in
The total garden for which
We in our green unfinished
Wisdom reach.

They are the faithfulness,
The living purely phrased,
Forever consonant
With the Praised.

## *Alvin Reiss*

### JACKSONVILLE: Bank*

Midnight hoofbeats down a sculptured street;
nitro and voices and spectral feet
scuffing over stones, over whispering floors;
a vault door hanging on blasted rust.
Nothin within
except the silence.
Accept the silence—
the gold has turned to dust,
the dust has turned to money.
Accept the silence, the redbrick rust, or flee
with empty saddlebags through a crossboarded gate.
The midnight you rode was an hour too late.

* Jacksonville was the site of the first gold strike in the Oregon Territory in 1851. A number of the town's buildings are as they were in the 1800s.

# *Thomas Reiter*

## PRUNING

1.

Honed by the emery texture of sidewalks,
his wheelbarrow's iron tire buds with light.
The local orchard has been pruned. All day
up Pennyroyal Hill he salvages
cord upon cord of no one else's fire.
His approach like the grinding of a blade
to both his sisters who were singing
in their brown garden. But they move now on their knees
with the silence of what they tend.

2.

And recall: yesterday among the arid,
ravelling orchids of the parlor carpet
he cried out to them what he called his shame—
that age had made of him a patriarch
of pensioners among the cool hush
of heirlooms from the father's wealth they'd all
outlived. *We do not understand,* they thought,
*We do not understand.* But for reply
the usual dust motes blossomed
and fell from the light, while the room
was conducted to repose
by the Old World mahogany grandfather's clock.

So then he buried its key in the arbor
where clusters of Concords hang like chandeliers;
he sat among rusting rakes and shears
in the toolshed until the gold rod
pointed like a compass needle.

3.

As cord by cord he attains the dusk
among begonia and dahlia stalks and vines
drying to a graph upon a trellis,
his sisters probe, untuned, for perennial
tubers. Trimmed of their hollow stems
they wait each winter in apple crates
in the damp cellar below the pendulum
rigid still as a tap root.

## *Dorothy Lee Richardson*

### WAKING AT NIGHT

Waking at night I feel the engine throbbing,
pushing dark waves away on either side;
a steady thrum – no stuttering, no stopping –
although the wind is strong, the ocean wide;
doing its business while I take my rest,
the intricate mechanism in my breast.

Many years it has labored thus without laboring,
smoothly holding our course. Yet ten years ago
I'd not have noticed what I now am savoring,
the sound of the pistons pumping the fuel's flow,
tired pistons more obviously now
pushing the juice that makes the vessel go,

and which in a few more years will cease and sink
through waves of dark closing over on either side.
We have traveled together so long it is hard to think
of swimming away from it on the untested tide

of an element I have never known before
toward a shoreless shore — —

## *Dionis Coffin Riggs*

### AN ATTIC FULL OF MAGAZINES

This is a day for clearing up
The attic. Wind is mousing leaves
Across the roof. Rain gallops over.

Magazines, magazines
Are making the old boards bend.
I must throw out the lot.

*Out West.* Aunt Henrietta,
Homesick for the East, had sent
Those here to even up the score.

Bound copies of the *Edinburgh
Review* that grandpa took to sea
Smell of old leather.

*The Outlook* with little faces
In the O'S. I had seen my mother
Draw them to amuse me.

I sit down with the *Bookman,* August
Nineteen-twenty-two, not long ago.
I know these writers, or I did.

William McFee on *Poetry
And Youth,* Arnold Bennett's critique

Of *Ulysses,* Edgar Lee Masters.

Deaf to the storm outside, I turn
The pages and remember years
Among my questing people.

I keep the magazines.

## *Elisavietta Ritchie*

### DACHAU NOW

Now roses grow there, fat with blood.
Well-fertilized with ash, strawberries glow red.
Children of eternal refugees,
phoenixes with ragged plumes,
roll hula hoops on ground long sanctified
by those one hundred thousand martyrdoms.
Their hoops are plastic halos, not for saints
but rather ordinary men
who long ago in their abandoned towns
brought bags of strawberries
or pallid rose bouquets
home to the family on summer nights.

The children glue loose petals to their cheeks,
stuff their mouths with strawberries,
then, dripping that pale acid blood,
wrestle for toy pistols in the dust
and, breaking hoops to fashion scimitars,
transform the sacred ovens into forts.

# *Margaret Rockwell*

## "A PRESENT FROM THE ISLE OF WHITHORN"

Gilt-rimmed cup, what can you give me anymore?
who am turned to drink emptiness.
The letters of your legend mock my mouth.
"A Present from the Isle. . . ." ah, tracery!
In the earth the gathered ones lie scattered like stones:
in your white body all of them were hiding.

Uncracked you are, unflawed,
a gentle porcelain
but in her last breath drained.

*The summers turn by Kildarroch*
*the falls come in by Burns.*

Her voice filled you, brim to overflowing,
your fluted sides to bulge
souvenir handled, brittle with such weights
and now you try to give, uncracked, unflawed.

In your white body all of them were hiding:
the chickens from Balhasie in the cart;
the trees that were cut down;
great-grandfather's prayer to plough the early day;
Andrew's oranges in the dooryard sun—

Oh, I was blessed
to know whose hand it was
held the spoon that tunneled
the porridge to the cream
in the shared dish with red and purple flowers!

Uprooted, they hold it in the blood like milk in a cup,
their children drink it all their lives long
learning from voices and the touch of hands.
But I receive responsibility
who never knew the voices and the hands.

Gone, gone the visions, now that her ghost goes
over the stony hillside, back to them.

*The winters go down by Kirkmabreck*
*The springs come up by Cults.*

At night, cup, from that distant isle there rises
in tint, in scent, in texture: very self:
heather of Whithorn I dream has come to cover
her white body where they hide no longer.

## *Jim Rorty*

### NIGHT HAWKS OVER BRONXVILLE

The night hawks fly all night over Bronxville,
Wheeling, dipping, ceaselessly winging,
Dropping their brief disconsolate cries,
Sky-drip of wild and ancient woe,
On the roofs, the greened gardens, the disheveled
dreams of Bronxville.

Did you know him, sky hunters, my friend who died
yesterday?
The fat man with the kind eyes, the hurt mouth?
Yesterday he tripped, hurrying for the 8:25;
Tripped over a leaky heart valve,

Stumbled into glory. Cry louder, sky hunters,
Cry, soar, as the freed soul soars,
This is my friend who had wings, but the world broke
them.
He was the carpenter's son in a Maine village.
He wrote trash for the ether waves, grew bald early
begot nothing.
This is the house that trash built, in granite mortised
and tenoned;
Bar in the basement, sundial in the court; each evening
he would fill
The bird-bath in the garden; the day birds knew him, but
at night
The crying hawks dripped woe and terror on his dreams.

Cry softly, sky hunters. Yesterday he tripped hurrying
for the 8:25.
They emptied his pockets at the hospital, his commuting
book
Had almost a month to run, but today
His seat in the club car is filled, the waiting line moved up.
Softly, sky hunters. This is my friend who had wings
but the world broke them.
This is my friend, freed now to fly and hunt again
The high pasture, the far fields.

## *Marina Roscher*

### THIS MORNING, ICE WAS

This morning, ice was
on the pond,
the kind that won't last

and only just hints
at winter
like sudden constraint

on otherwise lenient
faces. The
distance between leaf

and leaf had increased
on branches
since I last noticed

and it seemed the fence
was closer
to the house. I thought

that it looked as if
the church
and even the grocer's

place across the street
had folded
their roofs overnight

in a way that implied
changes to
come and another season.

## *Elizabeth Rose*

### COUNTERPOINT

Now let the mind rest
Here at the sea's edge
Out of the tide's reach
Bare as the dry beach.

Let no taut sail press
To mar the sky's reach
Out at the sea's edge
Far from the dry beach.

Here at the sea's edge
Out of the tide's reach
Safe on the dry beach
Now let the mind rest.

## *Nathan Rosenbaum*

### ON READING THE GREEK TRAGEDIES

Fixed upon the pages of this book
The poems are like creatures without tongues,
The words, in black on white, are ancient charms
Which ornament the marble breast of Time.

Then, as if by the mind's incantations,
They come to life, they open mouths, they sing
The sad, brief histories of men and women
Lost in antiquity, yet living here.

What is this illusion? Were these words
Written centuries ago? They breathe
With life, they speak with modern tongue, they tell
Of us who live, as once they told of them.

For we are much as they were long ago,
And we will be, at last, as they are now,
Fugitives between eternities
Who tell our tragic tales with little words.

The language of the heart is still the same,
The questions of the mind are still unsolved,
The flesh still has its joys and agonies,
And life is born in pain and dies in pain.

Here are the tragedies of human hearts,
The minds' treasons, the perfidy of fate,
And love that has its doom, and life its death;
Man against himself and against the gods.

## *David Ross*

### SPRING VENTS HER FUNNELS

Spring vents her funnels in the air,
Her circuit runs through man and grass.
The fires of her greening year
Were stoked from genesis.

Along my wrists revolve her wheels;
My flesh is cradle to her gear,
And I am road-bed to her rails,
My frame her thoroughfare.

I hear her birthing bell,
Clang like resurrection's din,
And I am the shaken terminal
Of her thundering green.

## *Norman Rosten*

### WOLFGANG AMADEUS MOZART

I invade the street, armed
With Mozart, and take on Commerce,
That greedy knight, all armored
In shiny welded gold pieces—
From fifty cents to ten dollars,
His visor a thousand dollar item
Forged by slaves at Fort Knox.
We battle it out, dodging
Between cars and funeral coaches,
I throwing some deadly tunes
From the F Major Quartet and Giovanni
At his head—they bounce off
And he stuns me with Stock Quotations
And Business Opportunities.
I'm breathing hard (we're on Wall St.),
Hugging the buildings, blinded by banks,
I let him have the Fantasia K. 475,
A chord gets through a chink—
Blood, thin and trickling! He's down!

O Wolfgang Amadeus, saviour,
I'm magic with you bubbling inside me,
Come war, famine, the Moon,
I've got you spooled safe inside me,

An endless joyous tape. I'm ready
For all comers, bless you, damn them
For having starved you to the end.

They take me in, book me on charges
Of creating a riot, assault and battery.
But we're safe, W.A. I swallowed
The evidence, let 'em torture me.
I crackle inside their handcuffs.
I'll tell nothing. I feel all.

## *Larry Rubin*

### THE BACHELOR

They asked me how I could die childless,
Seeing that there are no other claims
To immortality; and I was silent,
Knowing my head would spin with other skulls
In the world's old way, and all the poems

Would sift out on the air, like scattered
Ashes of some cremated soul. Creatures
Of dust (they said) must propagate to keep
Their kind embodied, and breath, not words,
Must mingle in that wet embrace—nature's

Remedy for dying. I rehearsed
My answer, prated of Platonic forms,
Supremacy of archetypes, transience
Of flesh—even that whose silken cells
Bear the magic label of your name.

Just then their children came to pull the sun
Down from heaven for a game they knew.
They asked my help, and I with wizard's eyes
Flashing within their woven circle, shaped
The holy words. The sun fell, and they were mine.

## *Ethel Green Russell*

### LETTER TO BASHO

BASHO, who taught you
The secret of seventeen
Magic syllables?

Or could it have been
The sun, the moon, stars, or wind,
Slant of April rain,

Bird upon a twig,
Petals fallen from the stem,
Seed within the seed?

Or might you have known
The greatest secret of all:
MIND within the mind?

## *Arthur M. Sampley*

### THE EPILOGUE SPOKEN BY A TAPE RECORDER

Though I am buried, I am on the air.
I was, in the strictest sense of the word, not there.
You would call me Eichmann, but I cannot bear
That appellation. . . . You may call me Zero.

I loved my children, I obeyed the laws,
I hailed the leader, joined in the applause,
I read the ads to see what I should wear
And bought the shirts approved for every hero.

I served the general and the general will,
Obeyed instructions, answered all my mail,
Killed only those whom I was told to kill.

I understood it all except the why;
They gave me names of those to put in jail;
They gave me orders for the ones to die;
I had my family to think of, I
Did not decide. . . .
                                        If anyone's to blame,
It was the leaders, but what could I do?
There were at first a few, only a few.
When millions died, I thought it was a shame.

They want to label it, to find a name.
I was condemned not by the law, but fate.
I was the man who happened to be there
When one state sought to try another state.
I was told, of all men, I was one to dare.

And I can see it as a tragedy

So wide it took three continents to frame,
And all of it was there except the heart:
The villain and the hero were the same.

The world is listening, I am on the air.

But if I did not live, I should not die:
They did not try me, but they tried the laws
That I obeyed. . . .
There was a nobler art
Lost somewhere in the scenes I helped contrive.
There was a better way, a fresher start,
And I have glimpsed at times my tragic part.

I died in it, but I was not alive.

# *George Brandon Saul*

## MENS DISCONSOLATA

Time being but consciousness perturbed to count
Its lunging footsteps, though it knows each lunge
Is but regression toward the dark whose seed
We furiously are: our tale a screed
Mystery has written and will soon expunge:
What have the years to offer but the brunt
Of disenchantment for the baffled heart
That did not seek its term, the strangled mind
That did not ask just power enough to spell
Its ultimate confusion, the mocked will
To beauty, though by agony defined?—

Little, indeed, except the blood-won art
Of love's endurance while the taut eyes crack
Against the flaming why of their grim zodiac.

## *Frances Higginson Savage*

### BIRD UNKNOWN

All summer long, some bird I vainly sought
beyond my garden wall, in a weedy acre,
sang on and on. Debussy might have wrought
such cadences as that small music-maker
wove to contrive the fabric of a fountain,
rain's flute-like dripping tones and semitones,
airy cascades of wind along a mountain,
and brooks, down-rippling lightly over stones.

Too well concealed for any to discover
in clumps of bayberry and elder brush,
he threw his heart at heaven like a lover;
and still my mind, in winter's deepening hush,
haunted by notes dissolved in feathered flight,
recalls his rapture on the edge of night.

## *Constance M. Schmid*

### JUNE NIGHT

They slept with the smell of the hay
fields all around them, June tired;

too tired to stay awake even for
the moon or the smell of the hay;
But it stayed with them
nevertheless, becoming part of them
as they breathed it in and out
not quite unconsciously, the livelong,
liveshort night.

## *Martin Scholten*

### KARMA

There is no reason to suppose
that accident will not at some
unforeseen moment
                    the sudden
bolt from high Olympus or the
devastating gnat in the eye
(hurling us out of time and all
the comfortable assumptions
we steer our courses by)
                              strike us
down—
          poor cogitating creatures
with neither Apollonian
oracles nor those proclaiming
our frailties to tell us why.

But in this a kind of comfort:
If driven to no marked hero's
stoic doom, though never without
awareness of our general
condition, is there good reason

not to sojourn by the wayside
for a moment's revelation
captured with the pleasure of a
face or flower?
                    It is thus we
achieve our singularity
before the inscrutable stone
masks—and so give meaning to the
landscapes we wander through beneath
the vast abstraction of the sky.

## *Morris Schreiber*

### OLD PRIMER

I stir four decades' dust on well-loved leaves
As Dicky Dare, young knight in knickers clad,
Sets out once more to match Sir Galahad.
From fowl-thronged fence, from snug-built nests in eaves,
Bold Dick is hailed, all Birdland's cheers receives.
—Look sharp! In sheep's skin wrapped to trick you, lad,
Waits villain Wolf. Soon furtive Fox will pad
Through silent moss, a chilling threat to add.

Serene at six, I crowned each peaceful day
When the lamplighter beamed his magic torch,
When Father came, high-buttoned, brisk, and gay,
Or Mother crooned old songs upon the porch.
—Lost world—in which my direst childhood fear
Was "Firehorse!" with the wild hoofs plunging near.

## *Myra Scovel*

### WOODSMOKE

Woodsmoke on an autumn afternoon,
    a bonfire, and the air like applejack,
eager tongues of flame that lick the spoon
    of brown leaf-batter and the crisp crack
of twigs the tint of cinnamon sticks. Soon
    three-thirty chatter and a bookbag's "thwack"—
the children, scarlet-sweatered from the cold,
tumble home from school knee-deep in gold.

## *Ruth Forbes Sherry*

### MOTIF FOR FUGUE

Where the bent wind intones on towers
of fluted stone, behold the sea's dark
dignities assaulted, still diminished
by the rock's tenure.

For here the sealed profundity
of time's annihilating mood
hollows the cliff with petalled wave
bequeathing coral reliquaries.

Mark how the lingual utterance
subdues the suave cave's rumorous
intent and answers to the bell's
distillate tone along the floor.

A Titan's heel half-hung with weedy
signature of earth's profound
resounds along the amorous wall
charges the tidal flux with music.

Spectered with storm the cormorant's
cry knells a gusty monotone
weaving in contrapuntal skein
the rhetoric of life and death.

## *Brant Shoemaker*

### SONGS TO THE BLACK MAN
Love and wrath

Let us
All be
Deeply
Men and
Women of
Love and
Wrath,
Kindling with
Might of
Dreams
Thundering
Yellow
Flames to
Char
Brute
Bigotry
To an
Ash,

And yet with
Gentle hands
Lead children
Far from
Such a
Stench,
Tomorrow's child
Asking,
"What is
War and
Prej-a-dis?"
Our
Answer being,
"Things of
Long ago—
Dragons,
Trolls and
Witches'
Brews."

## *Gene Shuford*

### TO TAME A GRIZZLY

The way to a little black bear's heart is sugar,
or peanuts, or a half-eaten sandwich, and if
you are adroit, you can make your amorous approach
by keeping the car window almost up
and poking food into the hungry maw
that rears up slobbering outside the pane
while tourists in other cars, clustered
like sodden flies along the highway,
admit the image of your daring

through the lenses of their cameras

(and not lose a hand

or even sacrifice a finger
to garnish the remains of the sandwich).

In dreams you tremble at night in your tent, hearing,
yet not hearing, the tread of big pads in the dark,
the garbage cans booming like tall drums,
the dark nostrils snuffling the night's black,
jaws grinding cast-off bones into blood.

In daylight a fragile pane of glass, at night
a spider's web of canvass between you
and insatiate hunger, terrible strength:
up in the granite mountains a great grizzly
smashes a bull elk with one paw,
rips the arms from two sleeping girls,
drags them to death among monolithic stones.

In the morning the sullen booming of rangers' guns.
And then, nothing—nothing but the stone prayers
of mountains waiting for our final silence.

## *William Vincent Sieller*

### THE TIGER DREAMS

In a realm both square and meager,
Caged and exiled, crowded in,
Curves the splendor of a tiger,
Alien beast in alien den.

Sun and grillwork stamp their markings
On his useless camouflage;
He is done with jungle lurkings
And his eyes are done with rage.

There he rests, a captive dreaming,
Moves a velvet serpent tail,
But in sleep outwits the scheming
Maharajahs on his trail.

## *Sarah Singer*

### THE MAD LIBRARIAN

How tall is light that stretches to the sun
Unwalled and free?
Forgotten now in wherefores and in whys.
This room makes finite all infinity,
Squaring the circle of each day undone,
And shutting out the pageant of the skies.
Lost, forever lost to me
The black-winged flight of clouds across the moon.
Locked in the mind,
The darkness merges with the afternoon,
Today with yesterday, before with soon;
Since walls are blind,
I cannot know how broad horizons are,
Or how the light is filtered from a star,
How time is hung in space and days divide.
My world is eight feet tall and eight feet wide.

I am lovely, I am lovely,
And my hair's the silken wing

Of a blackbird fluttering.
I am Lydia, Lydia Pritchett, I am lovely
And my name is like a bonnet,
Velvet crowned with feathers on it—
I am lovely in my bonnet
And my hair's a blackbird's wing.
But who is that keeps muttering?
Books? What books? There are no books here.
"Yes, sir, B shelf to the right."
(Your arms an engulfing hemisphere
To cradle my delight!)
And you, and you,
And you, and you,
Consult the file
For love's clear cue,
And dream hymeneal dreams the while
Of unlearned lips and shaken hair
Learned in a consummating night.
"Yes, sir, B shelf to the right."
(Within your arms I swoon and quiver,
Then awaken with a shiver.)
There are no books; there are no dreams;
these crushing walls are bare.

## *Knute Skinner*

### THE COW

There's a white cow standing upon the hill,
surely the whitest cow I shall ever see.
As usual with cows she is eating grass.
Nothing strange about that, except that the light,
the white light of the sun increases *her* white

until she seems like a moon reflecting the sun,
a cow-shaped moon newly materialized
to dazzle upon the rise of a grassy hill.
Perhaps she is the cow that jumped over the moon,
but how much grass can she nonchalantly bite
with that white light breaking upon her body?
O, now she raises her head and, striking a pose,
commands the field with a curve of her delicate tail.
And so I see that she has become a goddess
exacting and appreciating the homage
owed to a white spirit by darker creatures.
Those dull cows browsing in brown below her,
mere cows, I see that they cannot comprehend
how their appearance enhances the white goddess.
And yet their heads are lowered in due respect.
She is their deity as she is mine,
although I see her only from my distance.
I see her only through my grimy window.
Suppose I left my papers and left my desk,
walked through the garden, crossed the old stone wall,
slogged through the swamp at the bottom of the hill,
then with lowered eyes I could approach that whiteness.
Would I be touched to some extent by the sunlight,
and would my eyes be blinded with revelation?
Or would I find cowdung beneath my feet,
and would she and I eat grass for the rest of our lives?

## *Myra Sklarew*

### APRIL 1943

(there were three gifts:
a bit of earth, a bloody pin
from the leg of a girl, a dirty skullcap)

the head is a smooth stone
    when the flesh is gone
    the head is white

under the sun
    it is the living
    who are out of place

the darkness of their hair
    the strange motion
    while this dead one

reduced to her bones
    becomes a permanent part
    of the landscape

she is a carving of stone
    she is reduced
    to essentials

how her head
    is a smooth white stone
    under the sun

how her ribs hold the light
    how the legs relax in the bones
    the feet are spears

pointing under the sun
    the fingers forgive at her sides
    the toes are reproachful arrows

she is a carving of stone
    here it is the living
    who are out of place

# *Jocelyn Macy Sloan*

## ALWAYS THE SAME DREAM

Always the same dream—
packing up
with the urgency of flight,
of banishment.
It is near night,
near autumn, near despair.
We draw slip covers over
the furniture. Then she
folds her treasures away,
reluctantly.

I see again the hat box
lavender striped,
watch her take the Dresden
toys apart,
lift the shepherdess
from wreathed column,
bury her
in tissue paper,
layer after layer;
next, fragile and wan
do the same for the shepherd.
Looking on,
saddened by those transparent
fingers, I say,
"We can come and finish
this tomorrow."
"No," she answers,
certain that today
is her only time.

Outside a strange crowd peers
through windows no longer ours.

## *Hiram Lyday Sloanaker*

### HI THERE, MR. MAESTRO!

Step aside, Maestro! I prefer Beethoven;
Edge to one side, you are standing in my sight;
You are not a window, you are a door—
You are baffle and buckler against sound.
The dancing strings must detour around you,
The warm French horns tangle in your vest;
Sweet flutings feel at home in your column,
Your hair is full of hemidemisemiquavers.
Do not waltz, Mr. Maestro, stand you still—
Lead with the illuminating eye,
In motion minuscule move the smallest digit;
In slow time sway, launching the triumphant bass,
Crook one finger to unlimber those violins—
Aye, that's fine, fine! I don't see you now.
You are obscured by rising waves of sound—
The pure light of melody explodes in aureoles—
Beethoven and I, directly, now commune.
Let no mediator stand us between:
Ludwig and Hiram—Three makes it a Crowd!

## *Paul Smyth*

### AT THE PAWNSHOP WINDOW

I.

Dusk now begins to cool the boulevard,
Last sunset streaks high windowpanes uptown.
I stop to scan the pawnshop's caged display.
Ten years ago I had but small regard
For heritage, I pawned that hand-me-down
Gold watch grandfather smuggled from Bombay.
Here's Christ who said good losers would survive,
A painted plaster bust, five-ninety-five.

II.

When still half boy I lived five months alone
In a shack the wartime Coastguard jerry-built
To house a stove for the outer beach patrol.
I roamed the barren dunes, I heard that groan,
That howl, that silence I had always felt,
I wandered in the image of my soul.
How many years have passed since I would know,
If I dared try to return, which way to go?

I have no heart to dwell on all that's lost,
On fragile things I loved but trampled on
Crossing the space between my life and me,
And yet the heart is stunned at what it cost,
And still the heart returns to all that's gone.
My daydreams crowd the highways toward the sea,
And lately, in wild hurricanes of sleep,
My nightmares start in the surf and finish deep

III.

A cop now thinks: who loiters will trespass.
He starts across the street, his cautious gait
No less a dance for bullets on his belt.
I watch his formal progress in the glass.
Few words and we're agreed it's nearly eight,
Each thinks he knows just how the other felt.
Two men exchange polite brief pleasantries.
Newspapers scud and shudder on the breeze.

IV.

Pawnbroken Christ, the Spirit of an age.
Yet eremites still judge His price too steep,
Still scorn the common law of comfort lent
On visions that go unclaimed, still worship Rage
And scorn this Child of Rage whose mercy-weep
Has drowned the voice that bellowed Testament.
Pawn lust, pawn grief, pawn joy, pawn days then live
Eternal Life with all you've got to give.

In darkness at the ocean's bottommost
Grandfather still commands his drifting ship:
The rotten hull is carried on a tide
Of sand that moves too slow to please that ghost—
The Captain is wild to end this endless trip,
He rants his darkened curse, all rage and pride,
He has cleared the deck—mates, sailors, everyone—
And steers due east imagining the sun.

# *Daniel Smythe*

## FIRE STONES

Meteors are space's astronauts . . . at distances
in time they whirl to slash earth's northern skies
and bend into wrinkles of ash and nothingness
around the curve of a planet's atmosphere.
Such firefall is historical fastened on pages
lost in past centuries . . . I read somewhere
of a roof of sky lanced with the falling stars
so that people ran to watch the universe's ruin,
and how the darkness in the multitudes marched
arm in arm with ignorance, fearfulness, despair;
such a thing would not happen now; such firefall
would be worthy of speculation and wonder
and the blaze of knowing that from the regions beyond
Pluto
the meteoric astronauts discovered a dark world
and leaped into tightened seas of atmosphere
to claim their own . . . bits of lostness
come home like the dizzying Brazilian butterflies
whirling upon lightness, then extinguished by ocean.

# *Woodridge Spears*

## TODAY AT APRIL

The fox of heaven in the wind
At night,
And far away the singing horn,
The fox yet leads when ta-ra there

Returns the light.

No hunt to kill, the race to run
 This kind,
No ride to hounds in higher land,
But ear to hear the honey streak
Come up to mind.

The catch this time above the run
 To ground,
No thief this deal to sull and steal
And get, and set pace, a cold trail,
And horn to sound.

Who knows the season of this fox
 Knows well
The wind, and the dark of the moon,
What goes, and a patient long time.
It's he can tell.

Can tell the wish and say how long—
 The rain—
Today at April is, and all
To do, and laying off to try
That song again.

## *Lawrence P. Spingarn*

### VATERLAND, VATERLAND

A fifth cousin to my father (perhaps), he brought
The name, the stature, and the square cranium
By way of Hong Kong and San Francisco a century

Later, not too late. He saluted me briskly,
Fixed the monocle in his eye, barked an order
To sit down and drink a cup of lukewarm tea.
Beside photographs, his album held three locks
Of human hair, what was left from Auschwitz
Of love and family, but he pointed with pride
To the picture of himself, surrounded by men,
In the uniform of a *hauptmann,* taken in 1915
Somewhere on the Western Front. He wept easily,
Though we'd only just met, and asked in tears:
"What did I do that was wrong? Gentleman, soldier,
Good citizen—can you tell me, please?" Our tea
Was cold, the room buzzed with his questions,
But I fled the answers, blood on my shaking hands.

## *William Stafford*

### IN THE NIGHT DESERT

The Apache word for love stings
    then numbs the tongue:
Uttered once clear, said—
    never that word again.

"Cousin," you call, or "Sister" and one
    more word that spins
In the dust: a flake
    chipped like obsidian.

The girl who hears this flake and
    follows you into the dark
Turns at a touch, the night desert
    forever behind her back.

# *Ann Stanford*

## THE DESCENT

Let us, therefore, bend all our force and thoughts of
soul to this most holy light, that showeth us the way
which leadeth to heaven; and after it, putting off the
affections we were clad withal at our coming down, let
us clime up the stairs which at the lowermost step
have the shadow of sensual beauty, to the high mansion-
place
where the heavenly, amiable, and right beauty dwelleth . . .

Baldassare Castiglione

As I descend from ideal to actual touch
As I trade all the golden angel crowns
And rings of light for gross engrossing sense,
As I descend Plotinus' stairs
Angel, man, beast, but not yet plant and stone,
The sense of that height clings, the earthen hand

Transmutes again to light, is blessed from black
Through alchemy to rise rich red, green, blue,
Fractions of vision broke from ample crowns.

As I from the mind's distance fall on voyages
I test the strength of water where I walk
And lose the air for wings. I am lifted
As I descend past clouds and gusts of air
As I go down with wind to tops of trees
As I walk down from mountain tops and cold.

As I descend to gardens warm with leaves
As I enter the new morning harsh in sun
I count the earth with all its destinies

Come down to prove what idea does not know.

I descended out of nothing into green
I descended out of spaces where the spare
Stepping stones of islands roughed my way.
I descended into solidness, to dense
And mingled shrubberies where the birds
Alone choose wings for crossing my old sky.

Caught in this day within a sound of hours
Walled into shadows, stripped of multitudes,
I try this spring the climbing up to light.

## *Henry Stone*

### TIME'S KINDNESS HEALS NOT ALL

I locked a wound up in my heart
And went about my ways.
I did a multitude of things
The next ten thousand days.
I had occasion recently
To look into my heart.
(A matter had arisen
Which set my mind apart)
Then I knew why all I'd done
Was done as tho I mocked it.
The wound was raw and bleeding fresh
As on the day I locked it.

# *Dabney Stuart*

## THE RETURN

He'd had enough
Of the patterns of heroes
—The epic river
The descent into voices
The crisp symbol cast on a new shore—

Was done with disguises

Came home like any man
Stripped of his gifts
Derelict

And found the same door
He had always been entering

The same dead in the keyhole
The same shadows shaping the light
The same leak in the mirror

*My people* he said
And they said *My people*

The words danced on the threshold
Like grain in the wind
And when they bowed
He bowed

# *A. M. Sullivan*

## CONFLICT IN LIGHT

Seeing is not believing then;
The starlight lags from Time's frontier
And all that meets the eyes of men
Is yestermorn and yesteryear.

Patrol the lonely hour of sky
And what you see, from first to last
Is never the future's golden eye;
The starlight whispers of the Past.

The Pleiads drum upon the mirror
Of mountain tops much louder than
On Galileo's glass, not nearer;
There are three hundred years to span.

Light magnified is light. What more
Can ten times zero prove to him
Who stands on Time's retreating shore
Measuring the echo's interim?
Eight minutes since the solar lamp
Kindled this flame upon the pelt;
Eight aeons since Orion's camp
Blazed with the jewels of his belt.

Thought is instant. Light is slow
And cannot match the sudden mind
That circles all the realm of Now
And leaves the breathless stars behind.

## *Nancy Sullivan*

### HE HAS NO PERSONAL LIFE

Pedaling down the primitive road,
Pushing, pumping in a whiz,
He has no personal life.
The trees mesh above, so underneath
Night and day splatter on the ground
Shaping a dapple tent over the cruising man.
Under his hat, so camouflaged,
He merges with the road to color with the land.
Such signals in an hour: mailbox,
Fence, cow, tractor, bicycle with man
Flick onto the retina's clean spaces.

As the pattern from the trees tells
Nothing for a page, so this cycling man
Enters the mind as sun might.
He has no personal life.

## *Grace Tall*

### ADAGE FOR CROSS-STITCH

In the polished dewdrop
Dwells a speak of dust
And every golden muffin
Wears a suit of crust.

Through every dream that's woven
Runs a needled stitch

And inside every woman
Sits a tiny witch.

## *Florence Trefethen*

### MID-PACIFIC

My life divides at zero latitude.
Here is the middle place, the middle time
Of my itinerary. Left behind
By nine days' sailing is the bulk of my
Biography. All dates are in but one.
What waits ahead in my antipodes,
That second half, is non-statistical.

My clock stops dead for zero latitude.
Propelled at fifteen knots, I lie becalmed
On slippery sea. Long fallen behind
Landbirds, then gulls. Only the fish that fly
Can follow me. No shadow on the sun
Defines the albatross I will not see
Until I catch a wind to sail downhill.

Safe in the grace of zero latitude,
I alter course, renamed, baptized in brine,
My home soil rinsed away, cut free of lines
Once vital, still nine days from ties
To other shores. Sun plunges, gilds the rim
Of the hiatus that encloses me,
My limbo sea, time parenthetical.

My first night south of zero latitude.
The moon's inverted crescent starts to climb.

The Southern Cross is too far south to shine
On this horizon. Lights random in the sky,
Unmarshalled by the North Star. From the foam
Alongside, phosphor plankton signal me,
As once they winked Magellan on his way.

## *Eve Triem*

### A BOY DOWNRIVER

Along a river a boy runs
zigzag from the morning-bell: a dance
of bare feet slamming like books clapped shut;
a point-to-point hopping on flinty stones.

Stabbed by thorn, nettleburned, an animal
enjoying his muscles in the kill
of a snake. Finding in limestone cracks
*pasqueflowers* he drinks from a purple bowl.

The fun of being fish, clothes wet
to the bone! Away from the shiny bait
of honors in school! (I, I am river)
he lunges at berries, he breathes light,

dazed into torment and joy throwing
sticks at frogs, crushing the pungent snow–
yarrow and shouting dirty words–
a fertility-rite his nerves know.

Twilight. Hungry, young, afraid,
he returns to a world he senses is mad–
not really afraid but wishing for supper

and the silent warm meadow of bed.

A boy. A seed of wild power. How long
for a *sequoia* to grow tall; among
bronzed cattails for a hid cygnet
till the countable stars feather his wing?

## *Emma Gray Trigg*

### "POETRY IS FIDDLING"

*Poetry today is fiddling while Rome burns.*
Anonymous Critic.

"Fiddling while Rome burns"? So, indeed, it is!
Would you have Poetry put out the blaze
With smothering words and chemical sentences,
And blacken the glory with a deadly phrase?

No, Poetry would kindle a raging fire
In Rome itself, in every human breast,
Would blow the spark, would heap the fuel higher,
And fan the flame taller than Everest.

"Fiddling," you say. Can Poetry be dumb?
Its name is Singing, its own self is song.
In sound it mirrors this delirium
And celebrates this burning, right or wrong.

## *Vivian Trollope-Cagle*

### TEA TIME INTERLUDE

Someone said life was drum-shaped
stink stank stunk of lies lays and limbo.

Short-hair guessed it a shadow of clouds
grouped on the wind, soft as cat purr, really.

But Chigger argued life speaks it loose,
        but writes it tight,
full of scourging, thorns and vinegar.

Time leaned like a tired warlock
        on the witch of dunes
and seaweed swept the beach clean
it was that kind of day. The debate yawned
        in teams
whether the sky was yellow sackcloth
or a tidbit spread out like blue butter.

One intro and two extros, one flash of brilliance,
agreed that grasshoppers spit,
three ambis came up with dew—a dribble
from the chin of an idiot god.

## *Ulrich Troubetzkoy*

### DEER CROSSING

The brooms of light
brush night before the cars

that skim in elastic rhythm
along the road.
The signs loom up and sink—
*Speed Limit 60 . . . Keep Awake . . . Deer Crossing . . .*
*—but who can believe in deer?*

For the woods must be empty now,
so near to the city, so near to the highway.
The surf of the winds must wash through the empty
trees,
must seethe through the slippery pines
while the neon nibbles at moonlight,
and all the oak-rattling drowns in a whiny wheelwhir . . .
*—for who can believe in deer?*

Is he awake, the driver,
caged in his steel and plastic,
droning westward at seventy, lulled
by the Dow-Jones averages, the scores
of the Red Raiders and the Longhorns,
the far far awayness of Chou En-lai?
Is he awake in his soft rolling limbo?
The lights are raking the road ahead.
He almost thinks he sees
a tall deer plunging from the night of woods
into the scalding brightness . . .
*—but who can believe in deer?*

The brakes scream, the pale green glass
disintegrates like ice
against the many-pointed rack.

The driver stares into the moist dead eyes of his dream,
touches the wet shine of his own slashed cheek.
The antifreeze drips, splatters,
stinks like embalming fluid
as the buck blood leaks away

to the asphalt
in the almost instant allegory
of that hairline sight
where deertrail and turnpike
inevitably cross.

## *Virginia Lyne Tunstall*

### ALIEN

Where a man's roots grow deep, there should he tarry.
It is not good to wrest him from the loam
That holds the rich resources of his spirit—
The place his soul calls home.

A man disturbed, he will go sick with longing.
There is no comfort, though he wanders far,
Save in the spot belovéd and familiar,
Beneath one punctual star.

Meagre the happiness the world will give him.
Few there will be to mark it when he goes
To lie, a stranger in a world of strangers,
Under the alien snows.

## *Joseph Tusiani*

### SUNSET: A REFLECTION

There's some majestic sadness in the sun
which I detect and fully understand

in old men sitting in the dying light.
I look at them and recognize my land
still warm and fair yet ready for the night—
the night that wins and welcomes everyone.

I know what lingering flight is now less high
as I watch closely their inquiring gaze,
and as I try to listen to their words
I hear in every repetitious phrase
a tale that fledglings learn from weary birds—
from weary birds nostalgic of the sky.

I even see what brooks are growing thin,
and how much grass is left, half green, half gray,
above each hill and mountain of my earth,
as I examine on their hands of clay
half-freezing veins that sing no more of birth—
no more of birth when death is closing in.

Oh, but I have to live twenty more years
and suffer twenty centuries of grief
before I know what vision and what hope
can make my long existence look so brief,
and this last sun so sweet aslant a slope—
a slope where end my fervor and my fears.

There's some majestic sadness in the sun
if I have done with looking at the sea,
and done with watching every waning hue,
to know what will become of you and me
and what perhaps remains of me and you—
of me and you, dear life, so quickly run.

## *Wade Van Dore*

### EARTH WATCH

All is blindness where there is no understanding,
And it is vision that is needed now—
The close observation of desperate plants,
Starvation of voiceless flowers, and the throes
Of birds lacking direction to escape
These fields of poison. Blame blindness for
The lowering of the atmosphere's supply
Of oxygen, the transformation of water
From crystalline to cloudy—phenomenon
Presaging storm and black catastrophe,
The halt of man's priority upon
The breast of nature. Let those who see, see
Earth as a creature under great duress,
Panting, flapping like a captive butterfly.
What was said about *pathetic fallacy?*
Untrue! Stones, in a stone's way, are alive,
And it is rather man himself who is
Pathetic in his own made binding net
Woven of technological fallacies.
Escape could lie in the acknowledgement
Of the suffering of the earth. Then with late
Solicitude and hope, let us now stroke,
Not strike it with our forward tools, our hands,
And disentangle, gently, patiently,
The anguished, twisted chain of its ecology.

# *Mark Van Doren*

## THE FIRST SNOW OF THE YEAR

The old man, listening to the careful
Steps of his old wife as up she came,
Up, up, so slowly, then her slippered
Progress down the long hall to their door –

Outside the wind, wilder suddenly,
Whirled the first snow of the year; danced
Round and round with it, coming closer
And closer, peppering the panes; now here she was –

Said "Ah, my dear, remember?" But his tray
Took all of her attention, having to hold it
Level. "Ah, my dear, don't you remember?"
"What?" "That time we walked in the white woods."

She handed him his napkin; felt the glass
To make sure the milk in it was warm;
Sat down; got up again; brought comb and brush
To tidy his top hair. "Yes, I remember."

He wondered if she saw now what he did.
Possibly not. An afternoon so windless,
The huge flakes rustled upon each other,
Filling the woods, the world, with cold, cold –

They shivered, having a long way to go,
And then their mittens touched; and touched again;
Their eyes, trying not to meet, did meet;
They stopped, and in the cold held out their arms

Till she came into his: awkwardly,

As girl to boy that never kissed before.
The woods, the darkening world, so cold, so cold,
While these two burned together. He remembered,

And wondered if she did, how like a sting.
A hidden heat it was; while there they stood
And trembled, and the snow made statues of them.
"Ah, my dear, remember?" "Yes, I do."

She rocked and thought: he wants me to say something.
But we said nothing then. The main thing is,
I'm with him still; he calls me and I come.
But slowly. Time makes sluggards of us all.

"Yes, I do remember." The wild wind
Was louder, but a sweetness in her speaking
Stung him, and he heard. While round and round
The first snow of the year danced on the lawn.

## *Beren Van Slyke*

### ILLUMINATION

Through air and water, heavenly light
    Impels its virgin spark,
But man, of tougher substance made,
    Is fleshed with dark.

No sun transpierces his red blood;
    The body's somber seal
Is fortified by opaque bone
    From head to heel.

Yet in the eye such fire is banked
    Beneath the shielding skin
That it assures the night-filled heart
    Of light within.

## *Isabel Williams Verry*

### SMALL PARENTHESES

*He was a master poet and he died*
*a few years back,* I said.
And then above his poetry I read
the small parentheses of time
that bound awareness (his and ours)
of him.

Not twenty years!

Double that number blinked away from me
and fewer left for counting
until I become
eight digits calipered in stone . . . .

When did the trees divorce the spring
and hurl
their sloughings up the Highway of the Sun
upon this Great Divide?

No footholds here
where glaciers slide from laps
of hanging valleys.
Rivers are far
stampeding west . . . .

The bell has rung.
I close the book and move.
*Class is dismissed,* I say
and stand aside.

## *Charles A. Wagner*

### TO THE RULERS OF THE WORLD

Build colleges, not arsenals;
such armor has no peer,
the enemy has never lived
could vanquish an idea.

Spend all in algebra's defense,
heap high the table round
with learning, for the victory
is on that battleground.

It took a meek scholastic
with pure equative power
to calculate for all the earth
destruction in an hour

the logic of survival
presented to mankind:
build schools and universities,
stockpile the bomb of mind!

Build libraries, not missiles,
and let God's image grow;
there is no firmer way to peace
than thinking wills it so.

There is no weapon man can build
stronger than his own brain:
spend all we have for learning
or we shall all be slain.

## *Hamilton Warren*

### REQUIEM FOR MY FATHER

April,
        the time of arrowheads flown high,
        aimed at the Great Bear's heart. . . . .
and I remember.

You were leaning down, close to my cheek
and crying, "Over there! The geese! Over there!"
As flight after flight climbed morning
your grip tightened on my small shoulder.

When the last V blurred on the sky-line,
had gone, you were still watching the North,
your hands clenched, your head thrown back.
Puzzled, I looked up at your face:
it was streaked with tears.

Sleep well! Each April
that spring fletcher wounds me,
bringing you back, your awareness,
the Power and the Glory that, for you,
shone from those wings.

## *James E. Warren, Jr.*

### A DARK ODYSSEUS, UNCARING

A dark Odysseus, uncaring,
Calypso-clung
(all that bright bird-and-blossom cave!),
raft-clinging, riotously
flung
upon girl-screaming beaches,
pride-goaded into games,
and twanged to tears by harpers,
twanged to tears,
to tears —
such may disappoint us now.

Hold such in music, Homer.
Hold them in beauty and their languid loves
for our returnings.

Now must our heroes move more holily toward homes.

Cry up Athena!
Cry up old magic and good portents! Cry
up birds upon our right and clawing hate!

Be kind, Poseidon! Let our heroes plunge
more eagerly toward Ithaca and honor
until they come into their kingdoms' glory
and flourish more magnificently
their patient spears.

## *Irma Wassall*

### NOT BARE TREES

Not bare trees,
frost-blackened flowers,
nor deserted nests of birds
flown south;
not cold,
nor icy winds, nor fall of snow, have told
me winter comes to stay. Not these:
nor words
from any mouth.
Not these: but desolate hours
alone
I lie aware
of nights forever gone,
when your black hair,
not empty darkness, shadowèd
the pillow here beside my head.

## *John Hall Wheelock*

### NOT WE ALONE

#### I *A Garden and a Face*

The countryside that I love best is here,
And in this countryside a certain place,
And in this place a garden and a face
That in the garden sometimes will appear —
It is the gay face of the gardener, dear

Beyond all others, she it is will brace
The drooping vine-branch, grant the weeds no grace,
In the full green and glory of the year.

Great trees encircle her, her praise shall be
The thrush's song, the sea-wind for delight
Buffets her cheek while, massive in its might,
Around these island solitudes the sea,
Chanting, like voices from eternity,
Will shake the shore with thunders, day and night.

### II *So Dark, So True*

You turn to me with the old childlike, shy,
Questioning glance that first, in boyhood, took
My heart in bondage to those eyes — their look,
So dark, so true, be with me till I die!
From meadowy land, the meadow-lark's clear cry
Brings back, like something in an old story-book,
The days of our lost youth, and hours that shook
Their dear delight upon us in passing by.

Though these are ended, though life, that stays for none,
Must now flow on in others, shall we demur
That had such bounty of happiness from her,
In years together and hours that made us one!
Blessèd be they in whom life's ardors run —
Great life, whose temporary abode we were.

### III *Slow Summer Twilight*

Slow summer twilight. Darkening branches loom
Beyond the window. Your belovèd head
Bends over the pale page by lamplight, shed
Like a soft aureole round it in the gloom.
Kind destiny holds back the stroke of doom:

We are together, though no word is said;
We are together, and are comforted —
A peace, stronger than joy, fills all the room.

Outside, the darkness deepens, and I guess
What darker things the years may hold in store —
Watching your face, even lovelier than before
Age had given it this grave tenderness
Love stretches hands toward, that would shield and bless
A face, once young, in age loved all the more.

### IV *The Sea's Voice*

Our talk has been all banter, to-and-fro
Of raillery, the bland mischief of your smile
Still leads me on, with nonsense we beguile
An empty hour: we speak of So-and-So,
Of Eliot and Michelangelo,
And of James Jones, his high, pedantic style —
And touch, by chance, after a little while,
Upon some sadness suffered years ago.

Now your eyes darken, turning serious,
As thoughts of the long past, by memory stirred,
Waken — life's venture, tragic and absurd,
How brief it is, how strange, how hazardous.
Far-off, the sea's voice says it all for us,
Saying one thing forever, barely heard.

### V *Cloud-Shapes*

What huge phantasmagoria of cloud
And travelling moon works magic in the east!
Now gulfs of night, cloud-shapes of man or beast,
Grow bright or dim, with light or dark endowed
As the moon floods them, riding clear and proud,

Or pales, cloud-prisoned, soon again released –
Toward her they drift, diminished or increased,
Becoming now her mimbus, now her shroud.

Some night – and time will have annulled us then –
These things shall be once more: the moon will shine
Through shifting cloud-rack, casting silver-fine
Luster upon strange shapes of beasts and men –
And we not there to watch, ever again.
Come closer now, and lay your hand in mine.

### VI *The Letter*

The night is measureless, no voice, no cry,
Pierces the dark in which the planet swings –
It is the shadow of earth's bulk that flings
So deep a gloom on the enormous sky;
This timorous dust, this phantom that is I,
Cowers in solitude, while evening brings
A sense of transiency and how all things
Waver like water and are gliding by.

Now, while the stars in heaven like blowing sand
Drift to their darkness, while oblivion
Hushes the fire of some fading sun,
I turn the page again – and there they stand,
Traced by love's fleeting but victorious hand,
The words: "My darling, my belovèd one."

### VII *Bread and Wine*

We breakfast, walled by green, as in a bower;
Across the window-pane cloud-pictures float,
A trumpet-vine hangs there, a ruby throat
Glimmers, and is gone. Wind rocks the shaken flower.
The supper hour here is a golden hour:

Light gilds the treetops, eastward the remote
High clouds shine rosy gold, the oriole's note
Falls goldener, falling from his elm-tree tower.

Oh, in this green oasis here, we two
Together still – whatever fate provide,
To be together still! In humble pride,
I break the bread and share the wine with you,
Knowing, even as the disciples knew,
Love's very presence sitting at my side.

### VIII *In This Green Nook*

In this green nook and cranny hidden away
From time the ever-watchful, we have grown
Wiser in age, clung closer for our own
Defence against the inevitable day
When time shall part us, time that grants no stay
For natural grief's sake, which not we alone
Shall have endured, and questioned the Unknown,
That deigns no answer, question as we may.

The old inexorable mysteries
Transcend our sorrow: no mere discord jars
That music, which no lesser music mars –
It was enough to have made peace with these,
To have kept high hearts amid the galaxies,
Love's faith amid this wilderness of stars.

## *Ruth Whitman*

### STEALING FORSYTHIA

I came back with the sun smeared on my hands,
A yellow guilt
Pulled from my neighbor's bush,
Ten yellow branches
Moist with guilt and joy,
Caged in a green vase on the piano top.

Each time I pass my green and stolen prize
I feel again the greening of my years.

I would steal light from any bush,
Rob any blaze from heaven for my vase,
Just as I danced once on your wooden floor,
Naked and sudden,
Whirling you in a waltz,
Or did you whirl me,
Shaking the yellow spring
From rafters winter-stained with penitence?

That's the way I'd always have my guilt,
Sudden, high, a theft of fire, a dance,
A secret flowering of forsythia.

## *Margaret Widdemer*

### DARK COTTAGE

Few things trouble any more,
No need of grieving:

Darkened lights, clean-swept floor—
    Soon I am leaving.

What if there were once things scarred,
    Things lost and broken?
Soon are the doors fast-barred,
    Soon no blame spoken—

I shall run bright as day
    Past the black wood—
Wind will blow dust away
    Where my house stood.

## *Wallace Winchell*

### THE STORY OF MOHAMMED AND THE SLAVE

"Get down!" Abul snapped out. "I own you now."
"*God* owns me," the boy said. "I will not bow.
Only to God the Merciful I kneel.
What you command me, He does not allow."

"You worthless whelp!" Abul cried. Yet he thought
*Not a bad bargain this time that I've bought*
*from the slave caravan.* With kurbash raised,
he twitted, "By this lash you will be taught."

Bazaar crowds let their coins and curses fall,
haggling for wineskin, scimitar and shawl.
They did not heed the ridges like raw meat
in the black flesh. They heeded not at all.

A lash, another gash, a fever-swoon —

then like a rain cooling the heated noon,
one word braced up the boy as when the wadi
sparkles and sings all in a wet monsoon.

That one word, "Stop!" Slave and slave-owner saw
dread and inscrutable as Allah's law
a stranger come from desert silences,
his eyes a prophet's. They both watched with awe.

He moved as one who early risen to pray
comes when Athtar the morning star gives way
over Mount Ohod and the treeless sand
to the hushed edge of the pale veil of day.

The stranger said, "You know not whom you strike!"
Spike-toothed, spare-boned, Abul the human shrike
listened, his whip mid-air. "God in his image
made tradesman, sheikh and cameleer alike.

"God who has mercy in his very form
shaped from moist clay and mystery all who swarm
under the sun by camel route or sea,
each tribe of living souls breathing and warm."

Then Abul's fingers loosened limp with shame.
His whip slipped out never again to maim
Allah-in-man. He whispered, "Who are you?"
The stranger said, "Mohammed is my name."

I – al-Ghazzali – by faith an Emir
write: Let the Prophet's teaching stand out clear
*God made man in his image.* Let mercy be
the way of all men and each heart's desire.

# *Ann F. Wolfe*

## GIRL WITH WRISTWATCH

Sweetly to wrist you would leash this bird,
Make time a pet, pretty-pretty-please?
No girl has tamed God's ancient falcon yet,
Not Helen, nor Deirdre, nor Heloise.

If you'd play falconer, lovely fool,
To this skyling wild, this killer evermore,
Pause – on his wings is your soul borne.
Stroke no feather; let him soar.

# *Adrienne Wolfert*

## LIKE FOUR O'CLOCKS

Like four o'clocks, they flower once a day,
my black-eyed boys born in a starless night
who wear its beauty as their mystery.

Black
is beautiful,
a rainbow glistens on the blackbird's wing,
blue dusts the plum,
the moon makes mirror of the lake,
the tunneled earth
rich-dark
is studded with black diamonds,
a black fish darts
in irisdescent waters,

the treasured rarities
are blackest ebony,
the casket of black pearls,
the black fur of the seal,
the dark leopard's grace,
the jet butterfly,
the black flight of birds
and blackest night
which hides the sun of day
in radiance.

My black sons prowl
a forest without leaves
to hide them or dark stream
to give them drink or black
berry to stain their mouths
with summer.

I pluck
the orchid dark as jungles where
their fathers wander drugged to dreams.
I am
the trellis for their trembling faith,
not strong enough to hold the heavy grape
wine-black
nor waken rubies in their blood.

## *Stella Worley*

### UNIDENTIFIED CRAFT

Now the phraseological intellectual,
having captured poetry, stripped its wing,

cut its throat with whetted syllable
and thrown away its song,

burns its body at Minerva's altar—
perissology, abracadabra—and simulacrum
rising out of ash, a bloodless avatar
ballooned with idiom,

straining barriers of sound, goes
over the farm, the suburb, and city hall,
shakes the petals from a painted rose
framed on a duplex wall,

over haymow, harrow, and milking pail,
bevel, and welding torch, the thing flies
over the heads of hoi polloi, its trail
snarling the web of sky.

Bored by voluminous flight, the crowd
shrugs and talks prosaic matters, resigned
to loss of craft vanished in a cloud
by sleight of mind.

## *Olivia Young*

### HEAVEN, BLOW TRUE

Whatever is spirit color of wind,
the sea speaks back – as a violin
to delicate bow, as homing bird
to sun, as heart to wonder-word.

Isolate in this ocean-place –

not certain I will find the grace
of wind — myself in a heavy shell
that closets question; myself the cell
of listening fear, uncharted gust
of private storm I cannot trust.

I watch windwayward hurricanes
of sand caught-up like brandished flames
of loneliness. At line of sky
a solitary ship slips by
as if on glass. A haunting tune
follows a kildeer to far-off dune.

Yet, over over breakers rebound
with gloried hallelujah sound
spreading their iridescent blue
around my feet. Heaven, blow true!
Blow complex riddles from my cell;
let Jubilate fill my shell.
Blow true — as over a violin —
the exquisite equipoise of wind.

## *Marion Zola*

### ANOTHER TONGUE

As quiet tunes go everywhere unheard, unsung,
A listening few want passages between
Such goings and their own. Dreaming headlong
From the selfsame womb all melodies are sprung,

We shape toward synthesis what songs we know;
Solitude looms, an endless desert,
We move to leave it in a verbal flow,

Build bridges in the shadows of the mind

With words to cross it; though distances
Entombed with sounds and gestures have passed here,
No vehicles, deliverances
Have brought the kindred music any nearer.

But you, my friend, know other voices, places,
In silences escape muteness that bounds
Us all; over tortured wordy spaces
You leap without bridges, without sounds.

# *Jack Zucker*

## IN FLAT OHIO: A HYMN TO NEW YORK

I hunger in flat Ohio
For Sunday lights; for throngs gathering
In spite of dawn; for little cafes
With wrought iron chairs, bearded Negroes
Playing chess; for homos shopping daintily
Among Camembert, Tilsit, Cheddar, and Brie.
For spry Italian grocers (olives dancing
In pans, ricotta singing in tins);
For fat Jewish deli men (salamis swinging
From a trapeze of ropes, mustard swimming in
Three-quart tubs, pickles diving through cloves).

Sometimes, strangely, with divided heart,
I long for the bold, icy towers of steel and glass
That point high-logical fingers at the absence
Of God: in their humbling presence even boredom
Assumes the proportion of monument.

# *Biographical Notes*

ABBE, GEORGE, is the author of seven novels, of which *Yonderville* is the most recent. Among his seven books of verse is *Collected Poems.* He has also published plays and nonfiction, together with critical and technical studies. He has conducted classes at Mt. Holyoke, Yale, Columbia, Wayne University, the University of Pittsburgh, and Russell Sage, where he was for eight years Poet-in-Residence. He is currently Writer-in-Residence at State University College, Plattsburgh, N.Y.

ACTON, ELLEN, is a B.A. of Hunter College, where she edited *The Hunter College Echo.* Later she studied art at Fontainebleau and the National Academy of Design, before and after retirement from teaching at Jamaica High School. She has traveled and sketched in Europe, and has exhibited in a number of juried shows in this country.

AGNEW, MARJORIE LOUISE, a West Virginian, now resident in Maryland, was educated in her native Charleston. A contributor to the *Washington Star* and other papers, she is the author of a book of poems, *And the Moon Be Still as Bright.*

AIKEN, CONRAD, is one of America's most celebrated living poets and fiction writers.

ALBANESE, MARGARET is the author of *Heir to Eden* and *Fortune My Foe.* Folkways will issue shortly an LP album of her work. Her MSS are included in the collections of Syracuse University.

ALDAN, DAISY, a former PSA Board member, teaches creative writing at the School of Art and Design in New York City. She has published several volumes of her own poems, and has done notable translations of Mallarmé, Baudelaire, Rimbaud, and other French and Spanish poets, as well as from the German of Albert Steffen, famous Swiss poet and playwright. She is the recipient, among other honors, of the National Endowment of the Arts Poetry Prize, and the Rochester Festival of Religious Arts First Prize.

ALEXANDER, FRANCES, was born in Blanco, Texas. She took her B.A. at Baylor University and M.A. at Columbia, and is a teacher of English, Texas College of Arts & Industries, and the University of Texas and is a member of the Texas Institute of Letters. Her *Mother Goose on the Rio Grande* won a $2000 Scholarship to the University of Texas. A volume of verse, *Time at the Window,* took the $100 Institute of Letters award for the best poetry entry of 1948. *Handbook of Chinese Art Symbols,* written in collaboration with Mary C. Alexander, is an authority in its field. *Pebbles from a Broken Jar* was a Cokebury selection as the Best Texas Book for Children, in 1969.

ALLEN, SARA VAN ALSTYNE, a Phi Beta Kappa graduate of Pomona College, has had poems widely published, in *The Nation, The Saturday Review, The Yale Review, Harper's, The New Yorker,* and in the *Thomas Moult Anthology. The Steuben Poetry in Crystal Project* used her poem, "This Season." She was for nine years a Board member, and has been a frequent winner in the PSA monthly contests. The Golden Quill Press published her book, *The Season's Name,* in 1968.

ALTROCCHI, JULIA COOLEY, wrote the first book by a child of ten published in this country: her *Poems of a Child* (Harper's, 1904), for which Richard Ie Gallienne wrote the introduction. Her other volumes include *The Dance of Youth and Other Poems, Snow-Covered Wagons: A Pioneer Epic* (the story in verse of the Donner Party Expedition), *Wolves Against the Moon* (a novel), *The Old California Trail, Spectacular San Franciscans* (for Dutton's Society in America Series), *Girl with Ocelot* (Commonwealth Club 1966 Poetry Award), and other prize-winning works in poetry and prose.

ALYEA, DOROTHY, was a winner of the Rochester Festival, 1967, First Prize, and is a contributor of verse to numerous periodicals, including the *Chicago Tribune*'s "Today's Poets," and the *Ohio University Review.*

AMES, BERNICE, A.B., Wilson College, Pa., is represented in many well-known periodicals, and has had various awards and honors, including a Wrexton College, England, Fellowship (1967), a James Joyce Award, and an *Arizona Quarterly* Short Story Award. Her latest collection of verse, *Antelope Bread,* appeared in 1966.

AMES, EVELYN, born 1908 in Hamden, Conn., and a student at Vassar College, has contributed poems to many periodicals. Dodd, Mead & Co. brought out her first collection, *The Hawk from Heaven* (1958). Later prose volumes were: *Daughter of the House, a Reminiscence; A Glimpse of Eden,* the story of a month in the East African Highlands, and most recently, *A Wind From The West,* an account of Bernstein and the Philharmonic abroad.

ANDERSON, FORREST, is the author of six volumes and is represented in numerous anthologies.

ANDREWS, JOHN WILLIAMS, is Editor-in-Chief of *Poet Lore* and Director of the Cooper Hill Writers' Conference, East Dover, Vt. Since leaving Yale, where as student he was chairman of the *Yale Literary Magazine,* and as teacher a Fellow of Timothy Dwight College, he has been newspaper correspondent, lawyer, and government and public relations administrator. His books of poems are: *Triptych for the Atomic Age, Summer Solstice, Legends of Flight, The Round Earth Under,* and *Dark City.* Both CBS and the BBC have produced his radio scripts. His narrative Poem, "The Hurricane," was a joint winner of the Robert Frost Award.

ANGOFF, CHARLES, current President of the PSA, is Professor of English at Fairleigh Dickinson University, Editor of *The Literary Review* and Chief Editor of the Fairleigh Dickinson University Press. He is the author or editor of some forty books of poetry, fiction, biography, history, and criticism. His Polonsky saga, of which the ninth volume, *Season of Mists,* has just appeared, is well known. His three books of poetry are *The Bell of Time, Memoranda for Tomorrow,* and *Prayers at Midnight.*

APPLEMAN, PHILIP, Professor of Creative Writing at Indiana University, has published poems in many magazines, including

*Antioch Review, Arizona Quarterly, Beloit Poetry Journal, New Republic,* etc., and in Borestone Mountain's *Best Poems of 1967.* Byron Press, University of Nottingham, England (published his *Kites on a Windy Day* in 1967. In 1968, Vanderbilt University Press brought out his *Summer Love and Surf.* His first novel, *In the Twelfth Year of the War,* is a recent publication.

ASH, SARAH LEEDS, is the author of two volumes of poetry: *Little Things* and *Changeless Shore.* She is a contributor to many newspapers and periodicals, and has taught in the Atlantic City, N.J., public schools.

AVERY, HELEN P., poet and playwright, is a former book critic and interviewer for the *Boston Transcript* and *Houston Post.* Her verse play for children, based on *Snow White,* has been produced in Maryland, California, and Massachusetts. A director of plays in the Washington, D.C. area for the past thirteen years, she is currently President of the D.C. District of the American Educational Theatre Association.

BALDWIN, MARY NEWTON, a Ph.B., of the University of Vermont, past president of the Poetry Society of Vermont and Managing Editor of its magazine, *The Mountain Troubadour,* has had poems in many publications. For the past three years she has been at work on a bibliography and gazetteer of the state's poets and poetry from pre-Revolutionary times to 1940, a project for the Vermont Historical Association.

BÁN, EVA, painter, journalist, and poet, is official representative in this country of the Brazilian Press Association and foreign correspondent for Brazilian publications. A member of the Overseas Press Club and of the Academy of Letters of Rio Grande do Sul, Miss Bán has won awards in painting and journalism, as well as in poetry. Poems written in English have appeared in American magazines and newspapers, including the *Chicago Tribune.* A book of her poems in Portuguese, *Memino Verde* (Green Boy) appeared in Brazil in 1965, her volume of short stories, *Fear and Second Time,* in 1964.

BARBER, MELANIE GORDON, born in Anniston, Ala., is author of *Peace—An Ode for the Morning of Christ's Nativity,* with

Foreword by Nicholas Murray Butler, and of *The Third Anniversary—Dr. Tom Dooley's Vietnam and Laos,* now in its second edition. She is a former vice president of the Three Arts Club, a Life Member of the Art Students' League, and was an Official of the U.S. State Department's Cultural Relations Division, under whose auspices she traveled extensively in Asia during 1967 and 1968.

BARNSTONE, WILLIS, Ph.D., is Professor of Spanish and Portuguese and Comparative Literature at Indiana University; visiting Professor at the Universities of Massachusetts and California (Riverside) ; and Editor-in-Chief of *Artes Hispanicas.* He is the author, translator, and editor of numerous volumes, including *Spanish Poetry from the Beginning thru the 19th Century; Modern European Poetry; Eighty Poems of Antonio Machado; Sappho Lyrics; Poems of Exchange;* and *A Sky of Days.* His *From This White Island* was a Pulitzer Prize nomination for 1960.

BARR, ISABEL HARRISS, recently deceased wife of the composer, Conte Pietro Aria, was born in Texas. She taught at Fordham University and conducted a tutorial class in connection with the honors program. Author of five volumes of verse and two collections of one-act plays, she was the recipient of the Angela Merici Medal and the *Spirit* Award of Merit. For three years she served as president of the Women Poets of New York, and was for a double term on the PSA Board. In March, 1969, the opera, *Jericho Road,* based on one of her plays, with music composed by her husband, was produced by the Philadelphia Grand Opera Company.

BARZE, MARGUERITE ENLOW, is a free-lance writer who is cosponsor of the Ronald-Barze Poetry Group of Daytona Beach, Fla., where she lives. She is the author of *This I Give to You.*

BASS, MADELINE, was born in New York City in 1934. She took honors in English at Wellesley, where she was a Durant Scholar and Junior Phi Beta Kappa. Her M.A., earned at Harvard Graduate School of Education, qualified her as a Secondary School English teacher. She has also been active in civic and civil rights work. She was a featured poet in the *South and West,* Spring, 1971 issue.

Benét, Laura, member of the distinguished writing family and herself the author of more than twenty books of poetry and prose, is a graduate of Vassar. In early life, she engaged in social settlement work, followed by editorial writing on a number of newspapers. Her novelized biography of Emily Dickinson and her book of poems, *In Love with Time,* are among her latter-day publications.

Bennett, Gertrude Ryder, is the author of two volumes of poems: *Etched in Words,* and *The Harvesters,* which won the $100 First Prize for the best book in the Biennial Poetry contest of the National League of American Penwomen in 1968. She is also a two-time winner of the Arthur Davison Ficke Award.

Blackwell, Harriet Gray, born in Laurens, S.C., has her music diploma from Columbia College, S.C., and her B.S. from Teachers' College, Columbia University, New York City. She has written articles for many newspapers and magazines. Her poems have been published in the *Saturday Review, Ladies' Home Journal, Saturday Evening Post, McCall's,* and *Good Housekeeping,* and she is author of a volume of poems, *The Lightning Tree.* A new volume bears the title of *The Trees of Heaven.*

Blankner, Frederika, is a former Poet-in-Residence at Adelphi College, where she was founder-chairman of the Department of Classical Civilization, Languages, and Literatures. Michigan-born, she has a Ph.B. and M.A. from the University of Chicago and a Litt.D. from the University of Rome. Among her numerous publications are: *Pirandello Paradox, All My Youth* (poems), and *Art, Man and the Cosmos as Vibrational Design* (Harvard University Press, 1940).

Bloom, Robert, born in Newark, N.J., 1925, and a B.A. from the University of Chicago, 1954, is a part-time teacher, Board of Education N.Y.C., and part-time cab driver. He is represented in various verse quarterlies and anthologies.

BOWERS, HAZEL, born and educated in California, attended poetry classes at Columbia, and was poetry editor of *The Villager,* Bronxville, N.Y. A volume, *Cricket Voices,* is in process.

BRADY, CHARLES A., graduate of Canisius College and Harvard. is Professor of English at Canisius, and a book columnist of the *Buffalo Evening News.* He is author of fourteen books, including four novels, six children's books, and a volume of poetry. In progress are a critical book on the English Novel, two novels, and a children's book. Winner of the PSA first prize (1968) he captured the Cecil Hemley Award, 1970.

BRENNAN, JOSEPH PAYNE, born in Bridgeport, Conn., was, he says, self-educated. He served five years in the U.S. Army. He was assistant editor of *Theatre News,* 1940, and senior assistant of gifts and exchanges, Yale University Library, 1946. His stories, articles, and poems have been widely published in anthologies and periodicals, including *Best Poems of 1956;* H. P. Lovecraft's *A Bibliography;* the Alfred Hitchcock selection, *Stories Not For The Nervous;* the recent Doubleday Collection, *Haunting: Tales of the Supernatural, Great Occasions,* and *Every Child's Book of Verse.*

BRUFF, NANCY was born in Connecticut, but lived later in France and attended the Sorbonne. She has published five novels and a book of poems. Her latest novel, *The Country Club* (1969), also includes poems.

BRYANT, HELEN, born in England, is a contributor of poems and articles to *Poetry, The New York Times, The Christian Science Monitor, The Reader's Digest,* and *Pleasures In Learning* (N.Y.U.).

BUCHMAN, MARION, is a lecturer and teacher as well as poet. She has held positions at numerous colleges, including St. John's, Rider College, and the Peabody Institute of Music. She has contributed widely to poetry magazines, to *The New York Times, Chicago Tribune,* and other newspapers, and is represented in various anthologies here and in England.

CABRAL, OLGA, born in the West Indies, grew up in Canada and New York City, where she now lives. She has published two books of poetry: *Cities and Deserts,* 1959, and *The Evaporated Man,* 1968, and is anthologized in *Poets of Today* (International Publishing Co., 1964), *Where Is Vietnam?* (Doubleday, 1967), *Jewish Currents Reader* (*Jewish Currents,* 1966), *Poems of Protest Old and New* (Macmillan, 1968), and *The Writing on the Wall* (Doubleday, 1969).

CANE, MELVILLE, born at Plattsburg, N.Y., was graduated from Columbia College (1900) and Columbia School of Law (1903). In 1948 he received the Columbia University Gold Medal for excellence in both law and literature. He has published eight volumes of verse, and one combination of poetry and verse, *All and Sundry* (1968). His collection of prose pieces, *Making a Poem* (1953), now continues as a paperback and is used in school and college English classes. Mr. Cane was also an editor of *The Man From Main Street: A Sinclair Lewis Reader* (1953).

CANNON, MAUREEN, has published in *McCall's, The Ladies' Home Journal, Good Housekeeping, The New York Herald Tribune, Lyric, The Christian Science Monitor,* and *The Reader's Digest.* Her home is in Ridgewood, N.J.

CARPENTER, MARGARET HALEY, is the author of *Sara Teasdale: A Biography,* and a children's book which she illustrated, *A Gift for the Princess of Springtime.* She collaborated with William Stanley Braithwaite in editing a new *Anthology of Magazine Verse* (1958), and also edited David Morton's posthumous *Journey into Time.* She is a winner of the Greenwood Prize of the English Poetry Society (London) and a co-winner of the Arthur Davison Ficke Award.

CHARLES, MARY GRANT, Boston-born, lives now at Covered Bridge Farm, Dover, N.H. A graduate of Jackson College (Tufts), she received her M.S. from Simmons. Before marriage she was a social service executive. Her *Across a Covered Bridge* was published in 1958, and *Lambs of Lanarkshire* is scheduled for early publication.

CHERWINSKI, JOSEPH, of Lansing, Michigan, has published four poetry volumes: *No Blue Tomorrow, A Land of Green, Don Quixote with a Rake,* and *A Breath of Snow.*

CHUBB, THOMAS CALDECOT, is a graduate of Yale, where he won the John Masefield Prize. He has authored two important biographical works, *The Life of Giovanni Boccaccio,* and *Ariosto, Scourge of Princes,* as well as a number of poetry volumes, the most recent being *The Sonnets of a Handsome and Well-Mannered Rogue,* a translation of Dante's friend and enemy, Cecco Angiolieri, who figured in Boccaccio's *Decameron.*

COBLENTZ, STANTON, who edited *Wings, A Quarterly of Verse,* for twenty-seven years, is author of numerous books of poetry and poetic criticism, including *Time's Travellers* and *The Pageant of Man,* and has compiled several anthologies of verse. His latest poetry-oriented books are: *The Poetry Circus* (1967), an exposure of the frauds in recent poetry; a rhymed version of *Aesop's Fables;* and the book-length narrative poem; *The Pageant of the New World.*

COCHRAN, LEONARD, O.P., The Rev., Dominican Order of Preachers, assigned to Fenwick High School, Oak Park, Ill., where he taught English and Logic for seven years, is at present on sabbatical leave, studying for a doctorate at Loyola University, Chicago. From 1951–1955 he was in the U.S. Air Force, from which he was discharged with the rank of staff sergeant. His poems have appeared in *Spirit, Poetry,* and *American Haiku.*

COFFIN, PATRICIA, poet-artist, born in New York, lived in Europe until the age of fifteen, her father being in the U.S. Foreign Service. Her poems have had wide publication in such periodicals as: *Harper's, McCall's,* and *The Ladies Home Journal.* Two books are in progress, one city-oriented, one ecological.

COLE, E. R., born in Cleveland, Ohio, is a poetry critic of the National Writers' Club. He has also served as guest-editor of *Experiment: an International Review.* His work has appeared in various anthologies: *Contemporary Christian Poets, Best Broadcast Poetry, La Poésie Contemporaine Aux Etats-Unis,* and in many literary publications: *The Western Humanities Review, The Saturday Review, The Dalhousie Review, New Mexico Quarerly, Beloit Poetry Journal,* and others.

COLEMAN, MARY ANN, won First Prize in the Georgia Writers' Association Best Poem Contest, 1969. A contributor to various literary publications, she is represented in the anthology, *Rare Moments with Living Poets.*

COOPERMAN, HASYE, Ph.D. Columbia, former head of the Literary Dept. of the New School (1961–1967), and editor of World Publishing Co., she won the American Literary Association National Poetry Award (1957). She is the author of *The Aesthetics of Stéphane Mallarmé, Men Walk the Earth* (a book of verse), and of articles on classical Yiddish writers in *Jewish Heritage Reader,* together with a chaper on "Yiddish Literature in the United States" in *The American Jew, A Reappraisal.* Her poetry has appeared in *Beloit Poetry Journal, Voices International, Midstream,* and other periodicals.

CORNELL, ANNETTE PATTON, is a member of the staff of the Public Library of Cincinnati. Since her first sale to *The Smart Set* in 1928, her poems have appeared in over a hundred periodicals and newspapers. Co-founder and co-editor (with B. Y. Williams) of Talaria (1936–1951), editor, 1951–1953, her five volumes of poetry have appeared under the Talaria imprint. She conducts a Poetry Program for Station WCPO in Cincinnati, and was formerly poetry columnist for the Scripps-Howard *Kentucky Post.*

CORNING, HOWARD MCKINLEY, born in Nebraska, attended school in Central Ohio, and afterward moved to Oregon, where he began to write poetry. Soon his verse appeared in *Poetry, The Nation, The Saturday Review, The New Republic, American Mercury* and many other publications. His first poetry collection, *These People,* was followed five years later by *Mountain in the Sky.* In 1965 he received an annual award from the PSA. His most recent book, *This Earth and Another Country,* appeared in 1969. Mr. Corning lives in Portland, Oregon, where he is poetry editor of *The Oregonian.*

COUSENS, MILDRED, a graduate of Radcliffe with honors in English, studied at Harvard and the Tufts Poetry Workshop, and served a term as president of the Rochester Poetry Society. Now a resident of Cambridge, Mass., where she is a member of the New England Poetry Club, she has had wide publication in national magazines, literary reviews, and poetry quarterlies. She won the Gwendolyn Brooks Award given by *Approach* in 1963.

DABNEY, BETTY PAGE, born in Norfolk, Va., is assistant professor of English at Old Dominion University. She was educated at Randolph-Macon Women's College and at the University of Virginia, and is the author of *The Ancient Bond,* published by Dietz Press in 1954.

DARR, ANN, won the Discovery Award (1970) of the Poetry Center, 92nd Street, New York City. She was born in Iowa and received her B.A. from the University of Iowa. She belongs to Phi Beta Kappa and Zeta Phi Eta (professional speech fraternity), has written and performed radio scripts for NBC and ABC in New York, and has appeared on the Poets-in-Person Program of the International Poetry Forum in Pittsburgh, besides giving readings before many groups and colleges, and contributing to numerous periodicals.

DAVENPORT, MARIANA BONNELL, resident of Riverside, Conn., was born in Chestnut Hill, Philadelphia, and educated at Bryn Mawr (B.A. 1925). Her poetry has appeared in the *New Yorker, American Weave, Educational Forum, The Lyric, The N.Y. Herald-Tribune, The Christian Science Monitor,* and other periodicals and newspapers. Her book *Storm and Stars* was published in 1963.

DAVIDSON, GUSTAV, B.A., M.A., Litt.D., was Secretary Emeritus, honorary life member, fellow and consultant of the PSA. He was on the advisory board of the *Dictionary of International Biography* and was General Editor of the *Centenary Memoir-Anthology series.* He was author of a dozen books in poetry, drama, and angelology. In 1967 Macmillan published his widely acclaimed *A Dictionary of Angels.* His latest collection of poems, *All Things Are Holy,* appeared in 1970. Among his many awards, citations, medals, etc. are the di Castagnola $3,500 Award, which he won in 1967, and the presidential gold medal of the Philippines. At one time he served as bibliographer at the Library of Congress.

DAVIES, MARY CAROLYN, a lyric poet, whose verse has had wide magazine and newspaper circulation, is the author of five volumes, including *Penny Show* and *Marriage Songs.* Miss Davies was born near Spokane, Wash. and was the first woman undergraduate of the University of California to win the Emily Dickinson–Chamberlain Cook Prize for poetry.

DAVISON, EDWARD, the late, was a President of the Poetry Society of America, an eminent poet and educator.

DAYTON, IRENE was born in Pennsylvania and educated at Roberts Wesleyan College. President of the Rochester Poetry Society, she has published widely in the U.S.A., Europe, and Japan, and is represented in several anthologies. She won a Guinness Award in England's Cheltenham Festival. Her book, *The Sixth Sense Quivers,* is a recent publication.

DEFORD, MIRIAM ALLEN, poet and playwright, had her five-act verse play on Shelley published in the summer of 1969 issue of *Poet Lore.* She is the author of some sixteen prose and verse volumes. Her critical study of Thomas Moore, the Irish poet, was published in 1967.

DELAFIELD, HARRIET L., born in Quogue, L.I., served for two years as editor of the *Hampton Chronicle,* and in 1956 published a book of nature sketches, *Sea, Sand, and Soil.* She has lived in Saranac Lake, N.Y. since 1957, and is currently writing a column for the *Lake Placid News.* A field ornithologist, she is the Regional Representative of the Adirondack-Champlain area for *The Kingbird,* quarterly of the Federation of New York State Bird Clubs.

DE PIETRO, ALBERT, Professor and Chairman of the Accounting and Business Administration Department, Nassau Community College, has authored three books of poetry: *Moments in Passing,* (1967), *Sounds of Shadow* (1970), and *Island City* (1970).

DIMMETTE, CELIA, has a new collection, *The Winds Blow Promise,* published in 1969. Her previous work, *Toward the Metal Sun,* won the award of the Midwestern Conference at Chicago (1950).

DORN, ALFRED, PSA vice president, is the author of two volumes of poetry, *Flamenco Dancer and Other Poems,* and *Wine in Stone.* Founder-Director of the Rococo Association and of Baroque Press, he earned his Ph.D. from N.Y.U., where he specialized in Renaissance and Baroque Literature.

DREWRY, CARLETON, born in Stevensburg, Va., was from 1929–1949 Associate Editor of *The Lyric* magazine. He has lectured on poetry at Hollins College and has taught creative writing in the University of Virginia Extension. A past president of the Poetry Society of Va., he is at present a regional vice president of the PSA. He is also a Poet Laureate of Va. His work has appeared in numerous anthologies, and in the *Saturday Review, The Yale Review, The Virginia Quarterly, Poetry* (Chicago), as well as many others. His books are: *Proud Horns, The Sounding Summer, A Time of Turning, The Writhen Wood,* and *Cloud above Clocktime.*

DUNETZ, LORA, is a registered occupational therapist, connected with the Baltimore County Board of Education, serving physically handicapped and mentally retarded children. She has been a designer for women's publications, and for four years taught French in High School. Her poems are published widely. She is represented in Rolfe Humphries' Anthology, *New Poems by American Poets,* Vols. 1 and 2. A book of verse for children is in preparation.

EATON, BURNHAM, for eighteen years secretary of the New England Poetry Club, then vice president and president, is currently editor of *Writ,* N.E.P.C. *Bulletin.* A volume, *True Places; Selected Verse,* was published by the Golden Hill Press in 1955. Awarded the Golden Rose by the N.E.P.C., in 1956, The Lyric Leitch Annual Award, 1959, and its Memorial Prize for 1967, he has won a number of other national prizes.

EATON, CHARLES EDWARD, born in Winston-Salem, N.C., educated at the University of N.C., Princeton, and Harvard, he is a former professor of Creative Writing at the Universities of N.C. and Missouri, and a former Vice Consul at the Embassy in Rio. Author of four published volumes of poetry and a collection of short stories, he has been a contributor in this country and abroad to: *Harper's, The Saturday Review, The Virginia Quarterly, Poetry* (Chicago), *The Yale Review, The Atlantic Monthly,* and *The New Statesman* (England). His second volume, *The Shadow of the Swimmer,* was the winner of the Ridgely Torrence Memorial Award, and his third, *The Green-*

*house in the Garden,* was final nominee for the National Book Award. A fifth volume, *On the Edge of the Knife,* has just been published by Abelard-Schuman.

EBERHART, RICHARD, class of 1925, Dartmouth, is now Professor of English there, author of some dozen volumes of poetry, recipient of the Pulitzer Prize, Harriet Monroe Memorial, Shelley Memorial, and co-winner in 1962 of the Bollingen. Dartmouth, Skidmore, and the College of Wooster have honored him with Honorary Doctor of Letters degrees. Dr. Eberhart was Consultant in Poetry at the Library of Congress, 1959–1962, and a member of the Advisory Committee on the Arts for the J. F. Kennedy Center in Washington. He is a member of the National Institute of Arts and Letters and of the National Academy of Arts and Sciences. The Library of Congress reappointed him Honorary Consultant in American Letters, 1963–1969.

EIBEL, DEBORAH, educated at McGill University and Radcliffe, is currently teaching and studying in the Writing Seminars Program at Johns Hopkins. In 1965 her poem, "Homecoming," received the Arthur Davison Ficke Sonnet Award. She is a steady contributor to a number of leading scholarly and literary periodicals.

ELLIOT, JEAN, poet and free-lance writer, critic and historian, is a native of New York's Westchester County. In 1957 she and her husband, R. Sherrard Elliot, Jr., were members of the PSA's exploration party to Greece. At one time she was associate editor of the Bronxville Press.

ESLER, RICHARD CURRY, was born in Pennsylvania and after getting his B.A., at the University of Pittsburgh, and doing graduate work there and at Pennsylvania State, he was first published in Harriet Monroe's *Poetry.* He is the author of *Exits and Entrances,* (University of Pittsburgh Press, 1961), *Twenty Ballads Stuck about the Wall* (1967), *Travels with Cherry* (1970), and a book in progress, *The Fields We Know.*

FAIRBAIRN, VESTA NICKERSON, is President of the California Writers' Guild. Her poetry and light verse is widely published in domestic and foreign periodicals, anthologies and textbooks, and *Mild Silver and Furious Gold* was an early volume. She has taught creative writing and poetry at the University of California and conducted adult education classes.

FARBER, NORMA, B.A. Wellesley, M.A. Radcliffe, was born in Boston. She studied music in France, Germany, and Belgium, and in 1936 was awarded a *premier prix* in singing in Belgium. A concert artist, she has made many public appearances with orchestras and chamber music groups. Scribner's published her book, *The Hatch,* in their "Poets of Today" series, and Atheneaum brought out her verse fantasy, *Have You Seen The Narwhale?*. She won the PSA Reynolds Lyric Award, and the New England Poetry Society presented her with the Golden Rose.

FARNHAM, JESSIE, a native of Cleveland but lifelong resident of Cincinnati, won first prize in poetry in 1937 at the University of Cincinnati, which she attended at the time. Her work has appeared in *The Saturday Review, New York Times,* and other periodicals.

FELDMAN, RUTH, artist and poet, born in Ohio, was graduated B.A. from Wellesley. Her poems have been widely published in newspapers and periodicals, and her translations from the Italian in collaboration with Brian Swann have appeared in *The Quarterly Review of Literature and Poetry*. She has been recipient of prizes from the PSA and the New England Poetry Club.

FELDMANN, ANNETTE B., has been reading translations of her poems in France and here. For some years she has been working on a translation of the Parnassian poet, José Maria de Heredia.

FERRIL, THOMAS HORNSBY, born 1896 in Denver and a graduate of Colorado College, has published four volumes of verse and a collection of prose essays. He won the first $1000 Robert Frost Award, and has been a frequent prize winner, beginning publication as a Yale Younger Poet, followed by many other awards and honors, including the $10,000 prize for a play in verse, given by the Denver Post Central City Opera House Association.

FISHBACK, MARGARET, born in Washington, D.C., is a graduate

of Goucher College, Baltimore (B.A. and Phi Beta Kappa). She has been an outstanding writer of advertising copy and humorous verse in New York City since 1927. Author of seven volumes of witty verse and prose, her latest is *Poems Made Up To Take Out.*

FOGEL, RUBY, born in South Carolina, received a B.A. and literary awards from Duke University, and later studied at Columbia. She is published in newspapers and periodicals, and her first collection, *Of Apes and Angels,* was published in 1966. Louis Untermeyer's *The Pursuit of Angels* includes her "$E=MC^2$, A Sestina Proving The Equation," recipient of the 1966 Lyric Cummins Memorial Award. The following year, she was one of the three American poets honored at the Stroud International Festival of the Arts in England. She has recorded for the Archives of Recorded Poetry at the Library of Congress.

FORD, EDSEL, the late poet, was a consistent winner of prizes for his outstanding poems: the Ficke Sonnet Award, the Lowell Mason Palmer, the di Castagnola (for a work in progress), and the Dylan Thomas, all under PSA auspices. His book, *Looking for Shileh,* was a prize volume of the University of Missouri Press in 1968.

FOSTER, JEANNE ROBERT, the late journalist and poet, born in New York State in 1884, attended classes at Harvard. She was literary editor of the *Review of Reviews,* 1912–1928; was associated with the Quinn French Art and Book Collections, 1918–1924, and was American editor of the *Transatlantic Review,* 1924–1926. Her prize play, *Marthe,* was produced in Pasadena. Her several volumes include: *Wild Apples, Rock Flowers,* and *Neighbors of Yesterday.*

FOSTER, NELCHEN, born and raised in Louisville, Kentucky, studied voice and opera in France and Italy. She has contributed to the *Oregonian* and *Wings,* among others.

FOX, SIV CEDERING, is winner of the PSA William Marion Reedy Award and the Masefield Prize for "The Fiddler" in 1970. In that year she also won first prize for a lyric poem at the Annapolis Fine Arts Festival, and is published by such mediums as *The Chicago Tribune, The Denver Post, The Literary Re-*

*view, The Prairie Schooner, Poet Lore, The New York Times,* and many others.

FRANCIS, MARILYN, of Sedonia, Arizona, has her sixth volume of verse about to appear: *Rivers of Remembrance,* a narrative poem, recounting the journey into the Southwest survived by Hidalgo Antonio de Espejo. Director of Winged Arts Gallery in Sedonia, she has taken part in a number of poetry readings in the gallery's Inner Circle.

FRANK, FLORENCE KIPER, born in Atchison, Kansas and educated in Chicago schools and the University of Chicago, has contributed poetry, short stories, articles and book reviews, and drama to a variety of magazines and newspapers. The Provincetown Players, the Chicago Little Theatre, and others have produced her plays. Her books include *The Jew to Jesus, Three Plays for a Children's Theatre,* and *The Silver Grain.*

FRASER, HELEN LOVAT, one-time editorial staff member of *Woman's Journal,* London, is the author of two novels: *Tomorrow's Harvest* and *Fullfillment at Noon.* Her poems have appeared widely.

GINSBERG, LOUIS, is a resident of Paterson, N.J., where for many years he taught classes in English at the Central High School. Born in Newark, he received his B.A. and M.A. from Rutgers and Columbia respectively. His three books of poems are: *The Attic of the Past, The Everlasting Minute,* and *Morning in Spring.* He is represented in Untermeyer's *Modern American and British Poets.*

GLEASON, HAROLD WILLARD, was born in Boston in 1895. Educated at the Boston Latin School and class poet of 1913, as a Harvard freshman he won the Lloyd McKim Garrison prize. He was for twenty-seven years chairman of the Department of English at Kingswood School, West Hartford. An officer of the Hartford Poetry Club for many years, and judge of its annual verse contest, he was also director of verse contests at the Maine Writers' Conference. His poems have been published in more than a hundred periodicals.

GOODMAN, RYAH TUMARKIN, Russian born, came to this country at the age of four. Her first book of poems, *Toward the Sun,* appeared in 1952; two others, one for children entitled *Leaning on the Wind,* and the other, *It is hard to Speak,* await publication. Lyrics, written to music of her own composition, have been broadcast, and her poems have been widely published in leading periodicals.

GORMAN, KATHERINE, descended from pioneers who sailed out of New England in clipper ships, has had short stories, articles, and poetry widely published in this country and abroad. She has held state and national offices in the National League of American Penwomen. *Flesh the Only Coin* was a *South and West* prize-winning volume of poetry, and The American Poets' Scrapbook series chose her "Album" for publication.

GOTTLIEB, DARCY, B.A., University of California, and M.A., Hunter College (C.C.N.Y.), was former head of a private school's English Department, assistant editor at *Mademoiselle* and editorial assistant at Macmillan. She is winner of the PSA Dylan Thomas Award for 1966.

GRANT, LILLIAN, native Texan, writes: "I have studied with many teachers and experimented with many types of the written word; . . . Vivian Laramore Rader gave me a foundation . . . first privately, then at Huckleberry Mountain; among other teachers who have contributed, I must mention the late Elizabeth Stanton Hardy, and the very present Gilbert Maxwell." Represented in various poetry markets and with prose articles in Sunday supplements, she has a forthcoming volume at the Windfall Press.

GRAY, MAY, born in Kentucky, and educated there and in Illinois and Louisana, is a graduate of a business college in Arkansas, where she now lives. Co-founder of the Fort Smith Branch of the Poets' Round Table of Ark., she has conducted workshops, addressed writers' conferences, and published three volumes of poetry, besides giving private lessons in speech, art, and music. She has had many honors, such as First Place Award of the N.L.A.P.W. for an unpublished book, the PSA Dylan Thomas, and has been named Poet of the Present and Poet of the Year in Ark., and is represented in major anthologies and periodicals. She now has a children's zoo book and a new collection of poems in progress. A painter as well as a poet, her paintings have hung in many galleries and have been prize winners.

GREBANIER, BERNARD, educator, author, and poet, is Professor Emeritus at Brooklyn College. Among his numerous books are the recent *The Uninhibited Byron, The Great Shakespeare Forgery,* and the *Edwin Arlington Robinson Memoir* for the PSA. His verse, fiction, and critical essays have appeared in the major publications. He is a frequent book reviewer for *The New York Times* and *The Saturday Review.*

GRENELLE, LISA, former King Features daily columnist, has published three books of poetry: *This Day is Ours, No Light Evaded, Self Is the Stranger,* and has a fourth in process. Lecturer and workshop leader at Cooper Union and a number of schools and colleges and summer conferences, she has had wide newspaper and magazine publication.

GUNN, LOUISE, Assistant Supervisor of English and teacher of creative writing in Albany public schools, she is a contributor of poems to *The Christian Science Monitor* and others.

GURNEY, LAWRENCE has the unusual title of "Sea Serpent Observer" for *The Rocky Mountain Herald.* A geologist by training, he has recently concerned himself with mechanical and inventive matters and lapidary work. Born in Manila, P.I., he obtained his B.A. from the University of Southern California.

HALE, OLIVER is a staff member of the General Libraries of N.Y.U. as a researcher, assisting student research. He contributes to various university periodicals.

HALL, AMANDA BENJAMIN is a long-time member of the PSA, as well as of Pen and Brush, The Women Poets of New York State, and other groups. She has won many awards and prizes, and is the author of seven poetry volumes, the last two of which are *Frosty Harp* and *A View from the Heart,* in addition to several works of fiction.

HAMILTON, LEONA, widely published and anthologized here and abroad, is a winner of numerous prizes. A native Texan, she is a former president of the Tyler Creative Writers' Club. Her book, *Duel before Dawn,* is used in Spanish translation by Spanish classes.

HARGAN, JAMES, born in southern Indiana and educated at the Universities of Wisconsin and Colorado, is a Psychologist in private practice, and a contributor to numerous little magazines.

HARRIMAN, DOROTHY, is an alumna of Iowa State College, and did graduate work at the University of Pittsburgh. She has contributed to various magazines and newspapers, and was a winner in several college contests.

HAWKSWORTH, MARJORIE, born in White Plains, receiving a B.A. at Barnard, followed by graduate work at the University of California, is a teacher of creative writing and poetry appreciation at San Marcos High School in Santa Barbara. She was first prize winner in poetry at the 1966 Santa Barbara Writers' Conference, and is represented in the 1970 *National Anthology of Poetry.*

HAYES, DORSHA, exhibits in poetry her former prowess as a professional dancer early in her career, as recorded in the Library of Performing Arts, Lincoln Center. She has written two fiction and two nonfiction volumes, published here and in England and Argentina. Her *American Primer* was translated by Sigrid Undset and circulated underground in Norway during the Nazi occupation. She has lectured widely under Harold Peats's Management and B'nai Brith, and has published many essays on the subject of analytical psychology in official Jungian journals here and abroad. She is a former president of the Analytical Psychological Club, and a former member of the C. G. Jung Foundation. Only recently has she begun to publish her poems.

HEIMBINDER, B. A., born in New York, had a public school education. He contributes to magazines and newspapers and is author of *White Conquest—an Epic of Antarctica,* a verse account of the Byrd Expedition. He has also written several books for children.

HERNDON, BRODIE (Strachan), native Virginian, lives between Richmond and a summer home on the Rappahannock, with occasional trips abroad. He has been awarded numerous prizes, has published widely, and is President of the Virginia Writers' Club, as well as past president of the Poetry Society of Virginia.

HERSCHBERGER, RUTH, was given the Midland Authors Poetry Award for her *Nature and Love Poems.* Harper and Row published her *Adam's Rib,* a prose study of feminism, in the fall of 1970.

HERSHENSON, MIRIAM, as Chairman of the Writers' Club at Veterans' Hospital in Manhattan, edits the work of writing patients. Translator of the Yiddish poet, Mani Leib, she is also an amateur collector and occasional performer of folk songs. Miss Hershenson was a student at Brooklyn College and took special courses in writing and linguistics at The New School.

HIERS, LOIS SMITH, was born in the Kentucky hills, where she still lives. The Norfolk Prize, the Reynolds Lyric Award, the Leonora Speyer Memorial Award, and the PSA Annual Award of First Prize are among her numerous successes. Her book, *My House and My Country,* was published in 1958.

HILL, HYACINTHE, pen name of Virginia Anderson, was born in New York and is a resident of Yonkers. More than four hundred of her poems, short stories, and essays have been published. The New Athenaeum Press brought out her *Shoots of a Vagrant Vine* and *Promethea,* issued also by Scotland's Cameo Press. She is a PSA Board member, and is the recipient of a number of honorary degrees.

HOBSON, KATHERINE THAYER, born in Denver, was educated abroad; a sculpture student, she exhibited her work in numerous European galleries, including the Paris Salon. Her art studies continued in New York following her return to her own country in 1939, where she has become a well-known sculptor. Since childhood she had been writing poems, and now became also a member of a number of poetry societies, and commenced professional publishing.

HOLENDER, BARBARA D., native and lifelong resident of Buffalo, was educated at Cornell and the University of Buffalo (A.B. 1948). Her poems have appeared in *The New York Times,*

*The Chicago Tribune, The Jewish Forum, The Christian Science Monitor,* etc.

HOLLOWAY, GLENNA, born in Nashville, Tenn., an interior decorator and ghostwriter, began writing poetry six years ago, and with beginner's luck won a first place award of the Pennsylvania Poetry Society. The *Herald Tribune* published her first poem in print. A member of the Board of Trustees of the Georgia Writers' Association, she is preparing a volume of poems, and a collection of translations from the Chinese and Japanese.

HOWARD, FRANCES MINTURN, a New Yorker transplanted to Boston's Beacon Hill, won the first Borestone Mountain Poetry Award of $1000 for her first book, *All Keys are Glass,* published by E. P. Dutton, who brought out also her second, *Sleep Without Armor.* The New England Poetry Club honored her with their Golden Rose, and the North Side Arts Festival of Sydney, Australia, awarded her their First Prize of 100 guineas. The twelfth annual P.E.N. Anthology, *New Poems,* 1966, reprinted her "Childhood." which had previously won the Reynolds Lyric Award. Her poem "Testament" was the winning choice of the Rochester Festival of Religious Arts in 1970. A regional vice president for New England of the PSA, Mrs. Howard is also a member of the Executive Board of the New England Poetry Club, and a Borestone advisory editor.

HUGHES, DOROTHY, is author of *The Green Loving,* a Scribner publication. Her poems have appeared twice among the Borestone Mountain Poetry Awards, and she was represented as well in the *New Yorker Book of Poems.* Her poem "The Boathouse" won the PSA De Witt Lyric Award in 1969.

INEZ, COLETTE, born in Brussels of French parentage, emigrated to the U.S. at the start of the second World War. She has a B.A. from Hunter College, where she won several top poetry prizes. Winner in recent years of numerous awards, she has read her poems widely, including appearances at the Harvard Faculty Club, in New York City High Schools, and even in Manhattan cafés. She has been a PSA yearly contest judge, as well as a discussion leader, and is currently teaching English in a special Board of Education program. Several of her poems have been published in the Doubleday-Anchor anthology, *Some Poets of the Seventies,* as well as in Holt, Rinehart & Winston's *Live Poetry.*

INGALLS, JEREMY. Of her nine published books, four represent her work as a poet: *The Metaphysical Sward,* awarded a Yale Series of Younger Poets prize (1941); her major work, *Tahl,* a long narrative poem (Knopf, 1945); and two further collections of shorter poems, *The Woman from the Island,* (Regnery, 1958), and *These Islands Also,* (Tuttle, 1959). She has held a Guggenheim fellowship, grants from the American Academy of Arts and Letters and the National Institute of Arts and Letters, and many other foundation grants and awards including Ford, Rockefeller, Fulbright-Hays, and Republic of China (Taiwan) fellowships. Her other books are in the field of Asian studies and religion.

JACOBS, FLORENCE BURRILL, is a lifetime resident of Maine. Her published work includes *Stones,* a volume of lyrics; *Neighbors,* a 1949 Harper publication; and many individual poems in *The New Yorker, McCall's, Good Housekeeping,* and other leading periodicals. Winner of some thirty national first prizes, Mrs. Jacobs received the 1969 Grand Prix of the National Federation of State Poetry Societies.

JACOBY, GROVER, born in Los Angeles, was editor and publisher of *Variegation, a Magazine of Free Verse,* and *Recurrence, a Magazine of Rhyme,* both no longer published. He is engaged at present in translating poems for a series, *Translations: Comment in Motion;* a recent issue was *The Translation of E. Cevallos Calderon.* Mr. Jacoby is occupied with the American Alexandrine: "fluctuant, syllabic verse" in his definition.

JAFFE, MARIE B., retired New York City Public School teacher, specializes in translating from Yiddish into English, and English into Yiddish. She has authored *Gut Yuntif, Gut Yohr,* a collection of translations into Yiddish of well-known classics, together with original poems of her own. She gives readings for various organizations, and has appeared on WEVD and WOR radio stations.

JENKINS, OLIVER B., born in Boston, publisher-editor of *Tempo,* which later was combined with *Larus,* is a contributor to many periodicals, including *The New Yorker, Harper's Bazaar,* and *The Saturday Review,* and is author of three books of poems and a novel. Until recently he was political columnist for *The Boston Herald.*

JONAS, ANN, was born in Joplin, Missouri, and was graduated from Goodman Theatre in Chicago. Resident at Yaddo in 1968, she was formerly commentator, writer, actress, and producer for WHAS, Louisville, Ky., and interviewer-actress for WAVE (Radio and T.V.). She has contributed to many national and international publications, including a number of anthologies.

JORDAN, BARBARA LESLIE, a New Yorker before moving to Arizona, is a member of the Arizona Chapter of the National Society of Arts and Letters, and of the New York Women Poets. Contributor to national and international newspapers and periodicals, she is the author of two volumes of poetry, and a series of articles on India, Thailand, and Japan for the *Arizona Republic* 1959.

JUERGENSEN, HANS, President of National Federation of State Poetry Societies (1968–1970), has published six volumes of poetry, the latest being *From the Divide* (Olivant Press, 1970). He is Professor of Humanities at the University of Southern Florida, Tampa.

KAHN, HANNAH, author of *Eve's Daughters,* a book of poems, has had wide publication of individual poems, and has won a number of national and international prizes. She is a long-time resident of Miami, Florida.

KANE, DOUGLAS V., formerly in the Portuguese Consulate-General's office in San Francisco, recently retired from many years with the American Express, though still acting as a travel consultant for them. At one time he was Associate Editor of *Wings, A Quarterly of Verse,* and has published two volumes of poems: *Heart's Wine* and *Westering.*

KAPLAN, MILTON, Professor of English at Teachers' College,

and second chairman of the English Department, George Washington High School, was born in New York City in 1910. A graduate of City College and Columbia (Ph.D.), he is a contributor to *Poetry, Harper's,* and other magazines. His *Radio and Poetry* was published by Columbia University Press (1949). He is co-editor of *The World of Poetry,* and a former board member of the PSA.

KEITHLEY, GEORGE, of Chico, Calif. has completed a collection of poems, most of which have appeared in literary magazines. His "Charlie Chaplin" was first published in the Massachusetts *Review.*

KELLER, MARTHA, a native and resident of Pennsylvania, is an alumna of Vassar (A.B.) with graduate work at Stanford University. She had employment in publishing houses from 1925–1932, and is the author of three volumes of verse. Many of her poems have won awards and she has contributed to most of the leading periodicals and is in many anthologies.

KENNEDY, MARY, is the author of a number of books and plays, among them, most recently, *Ride into Morning,* a book of poems, and *I am a Thought of You,* adaptations from the work of a ninth-century Chinese poet. Two of her plays have been presented by Theatre in the Street. Her poems appear in leading magazines and anthologies. She lives in New York and is a member of several professional groups. Her play, *Shulo,* summer 1967 Theatre In The Street, was taken to Chicago for an extended run. *Come and See Me,* written with Helen Hayes, was published by Popular Library in 1967.

KILMER, KENTON, son of Joyce and Aline, was born in Morristown, N.J. in 1909. Widely published poet and critic, he has been clerk, Federal Housing Administration, 1936–1939; assistant to the Consultant in English Poetry, Library of Congress, 1939–1942; Poetry Editor, *Washington Post,* 1940–1947; Microfilm Reading Room, Library of Congress, 1953–1967, now retired. Editor of: *The Tidings Poets, vol. II* (with Frances Kilmer), 1944; *This is my America, Washington Post; The Congressional Anthology,* 1946, University Press of Washington,

D.C. and a number of other collections and anthologies. His own poems have appeared in many magazines and newspapers.

KOCH, JAMES, born in Milwaukee in 1926, is a graduate of Carleton College and also studied at the University of Wisconsin under Karl Shapiro, and at Princeton as a Woodrow Wilson fellow. Art and Copy Chief at Dun and Bradstreet, his poems have appeared in various magazines, and he has written poetry criticism for *The New York Times.*

KRENIS, LINDA, was born in New York. A Phi Beta Kappa at N.Y.U., she is on the Editorial Board of *The New York Quarterly,* and has published variously.

KRUGER, FANIA, long-time member of PSA, who was a native of Crimea, came here in 1909. Winner of a number of poetry awards, her poems and prose articles have had frequent publication in periodicals, and she has published two volumes of verse. Her *New Year of Trees,* a book-length poetry MS, was selected by Marianne Moore for first place in the New York Writers' Conference of 1956. Her work has had dramatic presentation on Texas Educational T.V. Her home is in Austin.

KUYKENDALL, MABEL M., book reviewer for the *Fort Worth Star-Telegram* and other publications, was former editor of *Quicksilver.* She is a radio reader and commentator, both in Fort Worth, Texas, and for Radio Station KKIT, Taos, N.M.; she has also done script writing and made T.V. appearances, in addition to her coast-to-coast lecture tours.

LABOMBARD, JOAN, was born in San Francisco, 1920, and took her B.A. in 1943 at the University of California. Her poems have appeared in *The Atlantic, Poetry,* and *The Virginia Quarterly,* and in Borestone Mountain Poetry Awards, where she took a first prize in 1959.

LAY, NORMA, writes a news column for the *Wellesley Magazine,* and notes for *The Chirp,* Ulster County bulletin of the John Burroughs Society. The annual Rochester Festival of Religious Arts booklet has twice selected poems of hers for awards and publication.

LE GEAR, LAURA LOURENE, a transplanted Texan in New York, where she raises show cats for T.V. and the movies while composing prize-winning poems, is the winner of many poetry awards, including a PSA Annual.

LENGYEL, CORNEL, born in Fairfield, Conn., lives in El Dorado National Forest, Calif. His published works include *Four Days in July,* the story behind the Declaration of Independence, selected by the State Department and translated into many languages, a portion of which appears in Untermeyer's *Britannica Library of Great American Writing.* Among his many awards are the Maxwell Anderson for poetic drama; the Maritime, the Poetry Society of Virginia; the Albert M. Bender Award for short stories, and a Huntington Hartford Fellowship in Literature. He was Poet-in-Residence at Hameline University in St. Paul, and a lecturer at M.I.T.

LENNON, FLORENCE BECKER, author of volumes of poetry and prose, published here and in England, including *The Life of Lewis Carroll,* is a well-known radio figure. She conducted for eight years the WEV Enjoyment of Poetry, a program broadcast over a number of stations. She lives in Boulder, and holds poetry classes in the student enclave of the University of Colorado.

LEPORE, D. J., born July 1, 1911, in Enfield, Conn., A.B., M.A., and L.H.D., is chairman of the English Department, Kosciuscko Junior High School, Enfield. Contributor to various periodicals, she is the author of a volume of verse, *The Praise and the Praised,* and a prose work, *Within His Walls.* She has numerous professional affiliations, including the National Council of Teachers of English, and The Authors' Guild.

LEVI, ADELE, born in San Francisco, A.B., University of California and student at the American Academy of Asian Studies, 1952–1953, is a social worker, a Service Supervisor for Aid to the Totally Disabled. Her poems are published in numerous periodicals and in the Activist poetry anthology, *Accent on Barlow.* She was given the 1956 Laramore-Rader Poetry Award.

LIEBERMAN, ELIAS, the late, was for many years Associate Superintendent of Schools, N.Y.C., and permanent chairman of judges of the Inter-High School Poetry Contests. His published works include *Paved Streets, The Hand Organ Man, To My Brothers Everywhere,* and an Anthology, *Poems For Enjoyment.* The Spoken Word Inc. issued a record of his poems. The Alumni Association of City College awarded him the Townsend Harris Medal for Distinguished Service, and the PSA named him a Fellow in 1960.

LINEAWEAVER, MARION, lives in Edgartown, Martha's Vineyard, and has sold poetry and prose since she was sixteen to every paying market. She has written several children's books, and adult stories for the "slicks," even "confessionals," and has won many awards. Poetry Editor of *The Writer* for three years, she was also on the editorial staff of *The Atlantic.* A teacher of fiction at Tufts University summer workshops, she has also taught verse technique at the Cambridge Center for Adult Education. She is the author of a verse collection, *The Season Within,* and is one of four authors of *Martha's Vineyard,* a joint poetry venture.

LINK, CAROLYN WILSON, Vassar graduate, is a native of Newark, N.J. and now a resident of Scarsdale, N.Y. She is the author of *Fir Trees and Fireflies,* and *There is Still Time,* the 1945 prize volume of The League to Support Poetry.

LINK, GORDDEN, as a college freshman in 1927, was brought into the PSA by Harriet Monroe and Corinne Roosevelt Robinson; twenty years later, while on U.S. Army active duty, he won the Lola Ridge Award for Poetry of Social Significance. Writing consultant for various federal agencies, he was the founder of the McCoy College Writers' Workshop at Johns Hopkins. *Three Poems for Now* appeared in 1953. After some years of free-lancing and editing, he was appointed Poet-in-Residence at Anne Arundel Community College, Md. and later at South-Eastern University, Washington, D.C. (1966). In 1969 he became Director of the Dellbrook Writers' Conference and Art Festival, sponsored jointly by the Center for Advanced Studies, Riverton, Va., and Shenandoah College, Winchester. His poetry has appeared in innumerable collections and periodicals and he has given poetry programs at the Universities of Delhi, Calcutta, Nanking, and Shanghai, and Durham University, England, as well as in London, Paris, and Athens.

LINTON, VIRGINIA, born in Philadelphia, had one year at Bucknell, followed by a stint as free-lance market researcher for Young & Rubicam Inc. and The Curtis Publishing Co. Her work is in leading periodicals, and her present poem tied for first place in the Poetry Society of Georgia's 1969 Critics' Award.

LLOYD, ROBERT, who was born in 1927 in Indianapolis, majored in German literature at the University of Minnesota. He served as photo-optical technician at White Sands Missile Range in New Mexico, and was Field Photographer for the Harvard-Peabody Museum-National Geographical Society Joint Expeditions in Wyoming, Early-Man Sites. He has been bar tender and chef, reading his poems in Claudés Santa Fé Bar, and was most recently research analyst for the Albuquerque model cities Cultural Programs Project, collating materials on Hispano-American and Afro-Latin-American studies and fine arts.

LODGE, EDITH, born in New York and educated at Oberlin College, Ohio, received her M.A. from Old Dominion in Norfolk, Va., where she lives. Widely published, she won the Irene Leach Memorial First Prize for a sonnet in 1964, and a *Lyric* First the following year. Her selected poems, *Song of the Hill,* appeared in 1964.

LOUIS, LOUISE, is a native New Yorker, Hunter B.A., author of *This is for You, The Dervish Dance,* and other poetry volumes, together with a children's book: *I See A Picture. Her Path to the Peak* (1955, 1956) is a collection of poetry dramas and tapes. A teacher's manual, *The Wonderful Becoming,* came out in 1963. A professional reader, she is a familiar figure on the platforms of teachers' colleges, clubs, and the Academy of Music and Art.

LOVINGTON, TED, past president of the Staten Island Poetry Society, is an alumnus of Wagner College, and for ten years was a high school teacher. He is at present a writer for the *Staten Island Advance.*

LUTZ, GERTRUDE MAY, a Californian, is poet, teacher, lecturer, and winner of many awards, contributor of poetry and prose to nationwide periodicals and anthologies. Author of several volumes of collected verse, her "African Sunrise" is included in *New Dimensions of Music,* an American Book Co. volume for classroom use.

MACARTHUR, GLORIA, born in Washington, former newspaper reporter, is now a resident of Miami. She received her B.A. from the University of Minnesota, is represented in many magazines, and has been honored with many awards.

MADSEN, MARION M., winner of the League of Vermont Writers' Poetry Award for 1968, is represented in such outlets as *Harper's,* and *The New York Times.* Last August she attended the Cooper Hills (Vt.) Writers' Conference.

MAGUIRE, FRANCIS, a New Yorker, is author of a volume of verse: *Journey with Music,* and contributor to numerous newspapers and periodicals.

MANSFIELD, MARGERY, a former PSA secretary and prize-winner, has published widely. Early in her career, she was business manager of *Poetry* (Chicago). Her *Workers in Fire,* a book about poetry, both in book form and on microfilm, has been reissued by University Microfilms of Ann Arbor, Mich.

MARCUS, ADRIANNE, born in Everett, Mass., and brought up in North Carolina, a B.A. and M.A. from San Francisco State College, she is a former poetry editor of the *Pacific Sun,* and is now a part-time instructor at the College of Marin. She is represented in a wide range of periodicals from *The Atlantic* to the *New Mexico Quarterly.* A resident of San Rafael, California, she "lives high on a hill in friendly isolation, not alienation."

MARMON, KAREN, a Radcliffe graduate now resident in California, has been associated with Mid-Peninsula Free University, and has been a member of a psychodrama troop.

MARSHALL, LENORE, a novelist and short story writer as well as a poet, is a Barnard graduate. She has published three books of poetry and three novels and made recordings for Spoken Arts.

Widely represented in magazines and anthologies, she finds time to be active in the Peace Movement, was co-founder of the National Committee for a Sane Nuclear Policy, and is board member of P.E.N., American Center. She has another novel and two children's books in progress.

MARTIN, PATRICIA, born and educated in New York City, has been publishing her poems since 1940, beginning in *The New Yorker,* followed by *Harper's* and other leading periodicals. She was poetry editor of the *Ladies' Home Journal,* 1952–1953, and Assistant Editor, through 1959. She has a book of poems in process.

MARX, ANNE, German born, published her first book of poems in German while still a young student. Since then, four collections have appeared here, and she has been the recipient of a number of prizes, including England's Greenwood. A member of the PSA Board since 1965, she is now a vice president, and has been on the staff of Iona College Writers' Conference since 1964, directing its Poetry Workshop. Her most recent volumes of verse are *The Second Voice* and *By Way of People.*

MASON, MADELINE, although an American poet, had her *Hill Fragments* first published in London, with Foreword by Arthur Symons, and drawings by Kahlil Gibran, whose *The Prophet* she translated into French. She was also the first American and the first woman poet to deliver the Festival Address at the 1953 Edinburgh Festival. She received the Diamond Jubilee Award of Distinction in Poetry from the National League of American Penwomen on the publication of *At the Ninth Hour: A Sonnet-Sequence in a New Form,* presented in MS at her Library of Congress reading, April 9, 1956. An earlier volume, *The Cage of Years,* has recently been reissued in paperback. Her MSS and recordings are at Harvard. Scheduled for publication are *Only by Love, Journey in a Room,* poems, and *As I Knew Them,* reminiscences. She was recently elected a member of the PSA governing board.

MASTERS, MARCIA LEE, daughter of Edgar Lee Masters, received a Borestone Mountain Award for her poems, *Impressions of My Father,* and has had other awards from the Society of Midland Authors, and Friends of Literature. She has published one book of poems, *Intent on Earth,* and has a fantasy, *Grandparp,* scheduled for publication. She has long been engaged in newspaper work and teaching, and is now Editor of "Today's Poets" in *The Chicago Tribune Sunday Magazine.*

MEACHAM, HARRY M., Past President of the Virginia Writers' Club, is chairman of the Advisors' Board for Affiliated Societies of the Academy of American Poets, and President of the Poetry Society of Virginia. His work has appeared in many periodicals and anthologies.

MENASHE, SAMUEL, born in New York in 1925, and infantryman 1943–1946, took his doctorate at the Sorbonne in 1950. His first book was published in London in 1961; his second in New York in 1970.

MERRIFIELD, GLADYS, Associate Editor of *Family Circle Magazine,* was already a prize-winner in her undergraduate days at the University of California, 1927, a year which saw her first published volume, *Sonnets Under a Roof.* She received the James D. Phelan Fellowship in Literature, 1935–1936, and her *Twentieth Reunion,* a narrative poem, won a Robert Browning Prize in 1947. Contributor to many magazines and anthologies, she is a free-lance writer of articles for a number of popular magazines.

MEYER, GERARD PREVIN, born in New York, holds a Columbia B.A. with honors in the classics, and an M.A. in English and Comparative Literature. As a student, he was President of the Boar's Head Poetry Society under John Erskine, and editor of *Morningside.* He has published two collections of poems, and a prose volume, *Pioneers of the Press,* widely translated. Adjunct Professor of English at Queens College, he has prepared many poetry and related programs for N.Y.C. station WNYE-FM and WNYE-TV.

MEYERSON, EDWARD L., a graduate of Northwestern University, studied also at Chicago's Loyola and The New School; conducted a Poets' Corner for a New Jersey paper and reviewed books. He is the author of four books of verse, and is currently credit analyst, tax accountant, and editor of a business publication.

MULLINS, HELENE, was born in New York, and convent-educated. Her poems in F.P.A.'s Conning Tower brought her nationwide recognition. *Harper's* brought out her novel, *Convent Girl.* She is represented in the principal anthologies, periodicals, and newspapers. A recent recording of her poems was made for Fairleigh Dickinson University. Her new collection, *The Mirrored Walls,* contains selections from three previous volumes, as well as many new poems.

MUNDELL, WILLIAM D., a Vermonter who formerly owned and operated a ski lift, is a skilled photographer and a regular contributor to *American Forests Magazine.* He was a winner of *Poet Lore*'s Stephen Vincent Benét narrative poetry award, and a volume of his poems, *Hill Journey,* was recently published.

NELSON, STARR, long a New Yorker, is now a resident of New Britain, Conn., where she has just completed a novel about a young Greenwich Village poet in the 1940's. Her volume of poems, *Heavenly Body,* was a prize-winner of the League to Support Poetry. *The Myth in the Vein* was her second collection.

NEWLIN, MARGARET, is a New Yorker, educated at Brearley School and Bryn Mawr, where she won the Gerould Prize for poetry and the Thomas for prose. Aided by two Association of American University Women fellowships, she received her Ph.D. at the University of Reading, England, and had her *Divided Image: A Study of Blake and Yeats* published by Routledge and Kegan Paul, followed by a second book, *Organized Innocence: The Story of Blake's Prophetic Books.* She has taught at Bryn Mawr, Harcum, and Washington Colleges.

NICHOLL, LOUISE TOWNSEND, has published eight books of poetry, the latest being *The Blood That Is Language,* published by The John Day Co. in 1967. She was awarded the $5000 Fellowship of the Academy of American Poets in 1954, and was made a Fellow of the PSA at its 50th Anniversary Dinner. Miss Nicholl is an Editor and Literary Adviser in New

York. She shared the 1971 Shelley Memorial Award with Adrienne Rich.

OAKES, B. H. is a Maine poet employed by the South Portland School Department for the past sixteen years. A charter member of the Poetry Fellowship of Maine, she is a vice president, recording secretary, and chairman of the Board of Review, on which she is currently serving. Her poems have been widely published and have won many prizes.

O'BRIEN, KATHERINE, A.B., Bates College; A.M., Cornell; Ph.D., Brown; Phi Beta Kappa, Sigma Xi, and New York Academy of Science member, is Mathematics head at Deering High School and lecturer at the University of Maine, Portland; she is also summer mathematics lecturer at Brown. Her additional honorary degrees include Maine's Sc. D. in Education and Bowdoin's L.H.D. An active poet as well, she has published in *The Saturday Review* and elsewhere, and has had a book of poems, besides her numerous papers in journals, including a booklet, *Sequences,* in Houghton Mifflin's Mathematical Enrichment Series in 1965.

OLIVER, MARY, was co-recipient of the PSA 1970 Shelley Memorial Award. Her first volume, *No Voyage and Other Poems,* was a 1965 publication of Houghton Mifflin.

PALEN, JENNIE M., President of Pen and Brush, and formerly of the Brooklyn Poetry Circle, is also a past president of the American Women's Society of C.P.A. Author of three technical books (one a college text) and a trio of poetry books (a prize-winner included), she is a constant contributor to leading publications of both poetry and prose, has won many national and international prizes, and is represented in a variety of anthologies. At present she is Associate Professor of Literature and Fine Arts at C. W. Post College, L.I.U., and holds its Litt.D. degree.

PALMER, WINTHROP, is Associate Professor of Literature and Fine Arts, and Trustee of C. W. Post College, L.I.U., whose Litt.D. degree she holds. Former drama chairman for the W.P.A. Four Arts program, she was director of New Haven's

New Deal radio program. She was Editor of *Dance News,* 1940–1950, and her poems, essays and translations have had publication here and abroad. A verse play, *Beat the Wind,* has had performances in various places, including a Southampton Arts Festival. *Like a Passing Shadow* is her most recent book collection.

PASTAN, LINDA, is a native of New York and a Radcliffe graduate, with her M.A. from Brandeis. Her poems have appeared in leading newspapers. Her first book is scheduled by Swallow for spring 1971 publication.

PENNANT, EDMUND, born and educated in Manhattan, has earned his living serving the children of N.Y.C. as a school principal. His poems have appeared widely in newspapers and magazines: *The New York Times, Commonweal, Antioch Review, American Scholar,* the *Literary Review,* and the *N.Y. Quarterly;* in a book, *I Too, Jehovah,* published by Scribner's; and in five anthologies. He is also a writer of documentary picture scripts.

PERRY, GRACE, poet, editor, and medical practitioner, born in Melbourne, Australia, was graduated M.B., B.S., from the University of Sydney, Australia. She founded the South Head Press (1964) and edited *Poetry Australia.* Her published volumes of verse are *Red Scarf, Frozen Section,* and *Zoo Houses.*

PETERS, FRANK, is a poet who writes: "I was born Sept. 14, 1927 in Sheboygan, Wis. Presently I am residing with my wife and two children in Glendale, Calif. I am employed as chief chemist, Los Angeles Division of Con. Chem Co. I hold no degrees nor have I ever received any awards."

PORTER, JENNY LIND, educator and poet, was born Sept. 3, 1927, in Fort Worth, Texas. Author of *The Lantern of Diogenes* and *Axle and the Attic Room,* she is a contributor to numerous national and international publications, and is chairman of the Department of English at Huston-Tillotson College, Austin, Texas. The University of Free Asia accorded her an honorary Litt.D. (1970) and she is a co-winner this year of the di Castagnola Award. Her articles on the slain president appeared in *John Fitzgerald Kennedy: Memorial Addresses.*

PRICE, NANCY, Cornell, B.A., University of Northern Iowa, M.A., has studied with Philip Booth, John Holmes, and George Starbuck. She has taught at the University of Northern Iowa, and has recently contributed poetry and prose to *The Atlantic, The Nation, The Saturday Review, The New York Times, The Virginia Quarterly,* and so on. She received the PSA 1967 Annual 2nd Award for her poem, "Merry-Go-Round."

RANDALL-MILLS, ELIZABETH, born in St. Louis, Mo., a resident most of her life in New England, lives now in Lyme, Conn. A Vassar graduate, she has collaborated with the composer Arnold Franchetti, in *Words and Silences, Country of the Afternoon,* and *Servants of the Altar,* a devotional, of which she is co-author.

REISS, ALVIN, born in Fort Sill, Okla. of a U.S. Army father and part-Cherokee mother, has authored fiction and plays that have had professional production, the most recent, *The Smallest Giant,* at Williamsville Circle Theatre in March 1970. At present he is a *Medford Mail-Tribune* (Ore.) staff writer, and News Director for ABC Radio KYSC. A resident of Oregon, he attended the University of Oregon and Southern Oregon University.

REITER, THOMAS, is Assistant professor of English at Monmouth College, West Long Branch, N.J., where he conducts poetry workshops. He contributes to some twenty literary quarterlies and has given readings at Upsala and other colleges.

RICHARDSON, DOROTHY LEE, is a former student of Theodore Morrison's creative writing course at Harvard. She was on the staff of the Cape Cod Writers' Conference and a winner that same year of a Robert Frost Memorial Fellowship to the New Hampshire Writers' Conference. Her *Signs at my Finger Ends,* a poetry chapbook, was the 1961 first award of the latter. She has recently won the $1000 First Prize of the *International Who's Who In Poetry* 1970 Contest. The *Atlantic, American Scholar, Ladies' Home Journal* and other leading periodicals have published her work, and she is represented in a number of anthologies.

RIGGS, DIONIS COFFIN, lives in an old Martha's Vineyard homestead of her forebears in West Tisbury with her husband, Dr. Sidney Noyes Riggs. She is a distinguished educator, lecturer, and illustrator, and has published two volumes, the first, *From Off Island,* a biography of her grandmother, who sailed the seas with her whaling husband (the John Lane English edition retitled *Martha's Vineyard*) ; the second, *Sea Born Island,* a collection of her own poems. She and Dr. Riggs have done wide traveling across this country and into Mexico, and she has twice appeared as a speaker at the Lynchburg Poetry Festival; her poems have been published in a number of well-known periodicals and newspapers.

RITCHIE, ELISAVIETTA lives in Washington, following residence in France, Japan, Cyprus, and Lebanon, with studies at the Sorbonne, Cornell, and the University of California, where she obtained her B.A. She has published three volumes: *Timbot,* a novella in verse; a translation from the Russian of Block's *The Twelve;* and a two-volume course for American University where she teaches French: *Readings in the French-speaking World.* A free-lance translator from German and Russian, she has two novels, stories, and a play in progress, and contributes stories, poems, and articles to numerous publications.

ROCKWELL, MARGARET, was born in Bridgeton, N.J., and educated at Bennett Junior College and Sarah Lawrence College. She lives in New Rochelle with her husband, a professor of philosophy, and their five children. Her poems have appeared in *The Saturday Review,* and in a number of poetry magazines.

RORTY, JAMES, born in Middleton, N.Y., and educated at Tufts College, was employed as an advertising writer in California and N.Y.C., and was involved in radical journalism until 1931, when he retired to a Westport, Conn. farm. In 1926 his *Children of the Sun* appeared, followed by many volumes of poetry and prose and a pair of verse plays. He has been an editor of *New Masses* and *Fortune,* and script writer for Voice of America.

ROSCHER, MARINA, born in Germany, took up residence in Florence in 1952 with her physician husband. There she published translations of poetry and prose, working on texts in many languages. Since 1955 she has been a resident of the U.S.A. Original poems of hers in English have been appearing in the *Beloit Poetry Journal, Epos,* and other periodicals.

ROSE, ELIZABETH, born in Buffalo and educated in private schools, was married at eighteen. She writes: "Since then I have gone it alone, reading, writing and studying. Ten years ago, during a productive poetry period, I had the good fortune to meet Madeline Mason and received my first professional help from her. Encouragement came in acceptance by the PSA, and I learned a lot at the meetings." She has had poems in a variety of magazines and in *The New York Herald Tribune.* For ten years she was editor of the Patients' Magazine at Northampton State Hospital. She and her husband have been wintering in Spain, but are settled now in Sharon, Conn. A volume of her collected verse is in preparation.

ROSENBAUM, NATHAN, a Philadelphian, educated at Central High School and Temple University, was on the staff of the *Philadelphia Inquirer* and *Evening Ledger,* 1917–1924; President of Colonial Trust, Wilmington, Del., 1930–1931; head of Rosenbaum & Co., Philadelphia, 1932. He is the author of *Songs and Symphonies,* 1919; *Each in his Time,* 1925, and three other poetry volumes. His collected poems, 1947–1967, appeared in 1968.

ROSS, DAVID, pioneered the reading of good poetry on the radio with his program, "Poet's Gold." He has also given public poetry readings at colleges and at the Library of Congress. In 1933 The American Academy of Arts and Letters awarded him the gold medal for diction on the radio. Ross' *Poet's Gold* Anthology has gone through several editions. His compilation, *The Illustrated Treasury of Children's Poetry* (Grosset & Dunlap), appeared recently. Winner of three PSA prize awards, Mr. Ross was created a PSA Fellow at the Society's 50th Anniversay Dinner in January 1960. He resides in New York City.

ROSTEN, NORMAN, is a former Guggenheim Fellow, as well as the recipient of an American Academy of Arts and Letters award. His plays have been produced on and off Broadway, and include *Mr. Johnson,* and his portrait of Emily Dickinson, *Come Slowly, Eden,* which was produced at the Library of Congress and at the Théatre de Lys by ANTA. Mr. Rosten recently completed the libretto for an opera under a Ford Foundation grant. His latest is a novel, *Under The Boardwalk,* and he has in progress a new novel and a book of poems.

RUBIN, LARRY, Associate Professor of English at Georgia's Institute of Technology, has just completed an exchange professorship, teaching American Literature at the Free University of West Berlin. Earlier exchange grants from our State Department sent him to Poland and Norway. He has authored two books of poems, both of which received awards: the Sydney Lanier from Oglethorpe University for the *World's Old Way,* now in a second printing, while *Lanced in Light* procured for him the title "Georgia Poet of the Year." *All My Mirrors Lie* is in process. Four hundred poems have had wide publication in periodicals and anthologies.

RUSSELL, ETHEL GREEN, born of Quaker ancestry on a Kansas farm, has published three books of verse, *Deep Bayou, Lantern in the Wind,* and *Land of Evangeline,* now in its third printing. She lives in Louisiana and contributes to magazines here and in England.

SAMPLEY, ARTHUR M., Professor of English at North Texas State, teaches a seminar in Modern American Poetry, and has published articles on Frost and Eliot. He was winner of the Edwin Markham Award in 1964 and 1965, and the James Joyce in 1969, the prize poems appearing later in *The Virginia Quarterly, The Antioch Review,* and *The Saturday Review.* He is widely represented in other leading publications.

SAUL, GEORGE BRANDON, A.B., A.M., and Ph.D., University of Pennsylvania, is the author of sixteen books and chapbooks. Professor of English at the University of Connecticut, he is a native of Shoemakersville, Pa.

SAVAGE, FRANCES HIGGINSON FULLER, poet and artist, was born in N.Y.C. and is an A.B. of Bryn Mawr, where she was an instructor in the English Department, 1922–1923, before becoming the wife of Howard J. Savage. She is a member of the Pen &

Brush Club, and is represented in leading periodicals and anthologies. She has four books of poems: *Bread and Honey, A Pinch of Salt, Winter Nocturne,* and *Postscript to Spring.*

SCHMID, CONSTANCE M., a Maine farmer, was born in the Bronx and has a Smith College A.B. Her Canadian father was a psychology professor at N.Y.U., her mother, a New Englander from Marblehead. She and her husband "farmed bitterly" for twenty years, but now content themselves with cutting and seasoning and selling lumber in their own business. There is still time for her to write and publish poems in the *Maine Times, Sunday Telegram,* and *Spirit.* Her hobby is nature study, especially watching for the woodcock's gyrations in the air, though as yet she has been "unable to view his acrobatic downward course."

SCHOLTEN, MARTIN, is associate professor of English at the University of Toledo, Ohio. He was born at Muscatine, Ia., in 1911 and was educated at the University of Iowa (B.A.) and the University of Michigan (M.A. and Ed.D.). His *A Later Shore* (poems) was published in 1951.

SCHREIBER, MORRIS, professor of English at New York Institute of Technology, was formerly teacher and supervisor in N.Y.C. Public Schools, from which he retired as principal in 1967. He is author-translator of several volumes of Folkways-Scholastic on poetry, the novel, short story, essays, and other aspects of creative writing. He has also prepared many scripts and teaching guides in the Popular Science Film-strip-of-the-Month series on world literature. Grosset and Dunlap published his *Favorite Tales from Shakespeare,* and *Stories of Gods and Heroes.* His poems have appeared in *The New York Herald Tribune* and *The New York Times.*

SCOVEL, MYRA, R.N., and her husband, F. G. Scovel, M.D., spent almost thirty years in the overseas medical mission of the United Presbyterian Church, seeing service in China and India, with a period of wartime internment by the Japanese. They returned to this country in 1959, and reside now in Stony Point, N.Y. Harper & Row have published three adult books of hers, including *The Chinese Ginger Jars,* issued in England and Germany as well, while half a dozen children's books have appeared under Friendship Press imprint. Poems and articles have had wide magazine circulation, and have been translated into Hindu, Urdu, Thai, and Portuguese. She has recently completed a term as N.L.A.P.W. President.

SHERRY, RUTH FORBES, born Nov. 14, 1883, was educated at Vassar, Stanford, and the Sorbonne. She has had many honors, awards, and medals, including the $1000 Olivant Award for her *Mojave.* Author of some dozen volumes, her works have been translated into Greek, Japanese, and French; she has had repeated productions of her dramatic poem, *Seize on Tragic Time,* and has given recitals to electronic music.

SHOEMAKER, BRANT, Professor, teaches poetry and modern literature at Pennsylvania State University, Ogontz Campus. He is author of three published books of poems, with a fourth in preparation. In addition to writing, he also paints, and his recent one-man show in Philadelphia was well received. His great-grandfather, he relates, was an "Irish slave" to a British landlord, which gives him a special understanding of such minority problems as that of the Black Man in this country.

SHUFORD, GENE, is the pen name for C. E. Shuford, chairman of the Department of Journalism at North Texas State University. His poems have appeared in *Scribner's, The Saturday Evening Post, The New Republic,* and other major publications, including anthologies. He won the Michael Sloane Fellowship Award, 1962–1963, and the William Marion Reedy, 1965–1966. His *The Red Bull and Other Poems* was a *South and West* Book-Brochure prize in 1964.

SIELLER, WILLIAM VINCENT, a native of Norfolk, Conn., is an alumnus of Buffalo University, and Canisius College, with a certificate of Advanced Graduate Study, University of Hartford. He is Associate Professor of English and Chairman of the Modern Language Department at N. W. Connecticut Community College, Winsted. Falmouth House published his first two books, and Golden Quill Press his *Green Water for a Granite Valley,* 1970.

SINGER, SARAH has published in *McCall's* and elsewhere, and is represented in Golden Quill Anthology. She is Poetry Chairman of the L.I. Branch of NLAPW and teaches creative writing at Hillside Hospital for the mentally ill.

SKINNER, KNUTE lives in Ireland when he is not over here teaching and lecturing in the Creative Writing Program of West Washington State College. He has given readings over a wide circuit of schools and colleges, has made recordings for Harvard, Leeds, and Hull Universities, as well as for the British Council and numerous radio stations. Represented in major publications and anthologies, he was a recipient of the Huntington Hartford Foundation Fellowship. Texas University has acquired his manuscripts for its Humanities Research Center Collection. He has published three volumes of poems.

SKLAREW, MYRA, M.A., (Johns Hopkins Writing Seminars) teaches creative writing at American University and George Washington University, Washington, D.C. A pupil of the late John Holmes and Elliot Coleman, she gravitates from the study of poetry to investigating the frontal lobe function of Rhesus monkeys, but has now returned to versification.

SLOAN, JOCELYN MACY, a resident of Rochester, is a practicing sculptor as well as poet. Her poems have appeared in such major periodicals and newspapers as *Poetry* (Chicago), *The Literary Review, Beloit Poetry Journal,* and others, including *The New York Times.*

SLOANAKER, HIRAM LYDAY, journalist and poet, is a former editor and book critic of the *Boston Sunday Post* and *Boston Sunday Globe,* and contributor to many leading newspapers and periodicals. He saw U.S. Army service in France, 1917–1919, and won the Purple Heart.

SMYTH, PAUL, is a member of the English Department at Mount Holyoke. His poems have appeared in *The Atlantic, The American Scholar,* and other major periodicals, as well as in many little magazines.

SMYTHE, DANIEL, a native New Englander, is Poet-in-Residence and Professor of English at Bradley University. His Ph.D. is from the University of Pennsylvania. Winner of many major awards, he has written three volumes of poetry: *Steep Acres, Only More Sure,* and *Strange Element,* together with a noteworthy prose book, *Robert Frost Speaks.*

Spears, George Woodridge, Ph.D., and Professor of English at Georgetown College, Ky., has had numerous honors and prizes in literature and history. Among his published books are: *The Feudalist, Elizabeth Madox Roberts,* and *River Island.* He is a contributor to a variety of periodicals.

Spingarn, Laurence P., born in Jersey City in 1917, was educated at Bowdoin College and the University of Michigan, where he took his M.A. in English, and is at present Professor of English at Valley College, Van Nuys, Calif. He has published half a dozen books of poetry and is represented in a number of anthologies, including *The New Yorker Book of Poems* (1969) and *Best American Short Stories* (1968).

Stafford, William, born in Kansas, was a laborer in sugar beet fields, soil conservation, and U.S. Forest Service, among other outdoor jobs. He has been active in a number of church and public service organizations, and, following high school and college training in the Midwest and as far northwest as Alaska, he is currently Professor of English at Lewis and Clarke College, Portland, Ore., with a leave of absence to be consultant-in-poetry at the Library of Congress for the 1970–71 school year. Recipient of such major awards as the National Book Award, Shelley Memorial Award, Guggenheim Fellowship, and Rockefeller Foundation, he is represented in many collections, and has had published some seven volumes of poetry and prose.

Stanford, Ann, is a West Coast poet, critic, and teacher, whose poems appear in major periodicals. Her published volumes include: *In Narrow Bound, The White Bird,* and *Magellan.* She reviews poetry for the *Los Angeles Times,* has taught at the University of California, and is now assistant professor and poet-in-residence at San Francisco Valley State College.

Stone, Henry, a New York lawyer who heads his own law firm, was born in New York City, educated in its public schools, and received his B.A. from the University of Pennsylvania in 1929.

After a year at Harvard Law School, he spent two years at Columbia Law, where he received his LLB. His poems in *Beloit Poetry Journal* inspired a letter of praise from Marianne Moore, her first communication to that publication.

STUART, DABNEY, a native of Richmond, Va. earned his B.A. from Davidson College and an M.A. from Harvard, where he was a Woodrow Wilson Fellow. His poetry has appeared in numerous publications throughout the country, among them *Epos, The Lyric,* and *Southern Poetry Today*. He teaches English at The College of William and Mary.

SULLIVAN, A. M., twice president of PSA (1940–1943, 1950–1952), was born in Harrison, N.J. and educated at St. Benedict's Preparatory College, Newark. For many years editor of Dun and Bradstreet's *Review* and *Modern Industry,* he also conducted the Radio Forum of Poetry over the Mutual Network. Counselor and lecturer, he has appeared before many educational and other groups. He has published many books, the latest being *The Bottom of the Sea,* 1966, Dun & Bradstreet; *Songs of the Musconetcong,* 1968, Guinea Hollow Press; and *Selected Lyrics and Sonnets,* 1970, Thomas Y. Crowell.

SULLIVAN, NANCY, is Professor of English at Rhode Island College in Providence. Her *The History of the World as Pictures* won the 1965 Devins Award, and her *Perspective and the Poetic Process* was a Mouton 1968 publication. Her poems and reviews have appeared in many major publications.

TALL, GRACE, born in Neponsit, L.I., is now a resident of Montrose, N.Y. She was educated at N.Y.U., and Chestnut Hill College, Phila., where she was graduated, B.A. in 1941. Mother of two children, she is a regular contributor to a Westchester County newspaper.

TREFETHEN, FLORENCE, former Professor of English at Girton College, Cambridge, Tufts University, Northeastern University, and Radcliffe Seminars, she works as a free-lance editor and writer. Her column, "The Poet Works," is a bi-weekly feature of *The Writer,* under whose imprint her book for beginning poets, *Writing a Poem,* appeared.

TRIEM, EVE, has had thirty-three years of magazine publication, representation in major anthologies, and readings and lectures from coast to coast, culminating in major prizes, the most recent and most important being a grant from the National Endowment for the Arts, 1969, following a National Institute of Arts and Letters Prize, 1966. Among her published books are: *Parade of Doves,* a League To Support Poetry (1946) award; *Poems* (1965) ; *Heliodora,* translations from The Greek Anthology, 1968; and *e. e. cummings, a monograph,* for the Minnesota Press in 1969.

TRIGG, EMMA GRAY, a resident of Richmond, Va., studied at Columbia University and the University of Virginia, and, though not graduated, is an honorary member of the Association of University Women. One of the founders of the Richmond Symphony Orchestra, she is a former vice president, and a present member, of the Board. Her poems have won many awards. The Golden Quill Press recently issued her *Paulonia Tree.*

TROLLOPE-CAGLE, VIVIAN JEWEL, lives in Las Vegas, Nev., where she receives many medals and honors from abroad in recognition of her contribution to poetry; included are an Hon. Doctorate from the International Academy of Leadership of the Philippines, a gold medal from the International Poets Shrine in Calif., and the most recent, an honorary doctorate from L'Université Libre d'Asie, Pakistan. She resigned a short time ago as Contest Chairman of the American Poetry League, due to a sudden loss of sight, and is now enrolled at the Sightless Center, reading and transcribing Braille. Born in Kansas, she is descended from the English Lockes and Trollopes.

TROUBETZKOY, ULRICH, immediate Past President, National Federation of Press Women, former chairman Citizens' Committee on the Status of Women in Virginia, candidate for Congress from the Third District, has been journalist (*Richmond News-Leader* feature writer and columnist), teacher of creative writing (Virginia Commonwealth University), editor (*Virginia Cavalcade,* and assistant editor, *Virginia Wildlife*), and ETV broadcaster ("Shapes and Sounds of Poetry"—WCVE). She is a winner of the Freedom Foundation's George Washington medal, recipient of many other national and regional awards for literature, journalism, history, radio, and T.V., and has written five books, including two award volumes, *Out of the Wilderness* and *Sagamore Creek.*

TUNSTALL, VIRGINIA LYNE, was one of the founders of *The Lyric: A Magazine of Verse* in 1921, and for some years was its associate editor. A resident of Norfolk, Va., she was elected an honorary member of Phi Beta Kappa, Alpha Chapter, College of William and Mary, in 1931. She is a trustee of the Norfolk Museum of Arts and Sciences, and is the author of *A White Sail Set,* a book of poems.

TUSIANI, JOSEPH, Professor of Romance Languages at the College of Mount St. Vincent, in New York, has recorded his poems for the Library of Congress, and is represented in the Borestone Mountain awards: *Best Poems of 1965.* He has had the Greenwood Prize, 1956; the di Castagnola Award, 1968; and the gold medal of *Spirit.* The notable translator of *The Complete Poems of Michelangelo,* and of Tasso's *Jerusalem Delivered,* he has published two volumes of his own verse: *Rind and All,* and *The Fifth Season.*

VAN DORE, WADE, born Dec. 12, 1899, was Poet-In-Residence at Marlboro College, Vt. in 1950, and is a recent recipient of the di Castagnola Award. He contributes poems to many major periodicals. Currently he is at work on a volume of reminiscence based on his long friendship with Robert Frost.

VAN DOREN, MARK, was born in Illinois, Jan. 13, 1894. Pulitzer Prize winner and one of America's leading men of letters, he is a former editor of *The Nation,* Past President of the American Academy of Arts and Letters, Lifetime professor of English at Columbia University, and recipient of numberless awards, including the Annual Creativity Award of the Huntington Hartford Foundation, the Emerson-Thoreau Award of the American Academy of Arts and Sciences, the Brotherhood Award of the National Conference of Christians and Jews, Columbia's Alexander Hamilton medal, and the PSA Alexander Droutzkoy gold medal. Among his volumes of verse, biography, critical studies, plays and novels, are *Shakespeare, The Hayfield Deer, The Last*

*Days of Lincoln, The Happy Critic,* and *The Narrative Poems of Mark Van Doren.*

Van Slyke, Beren, born in Fort Wayne, Ind., in 1891, lives now in Valley Cottage, N.Y. A Wellesley B.A. she has published two novels: *Power of the Sun,* and *This Was Sandra.* She won the 1968 PSA annual First Prize with "Provençal Donkey at Evening."

Verry, Isabel Williams, a resident of Memphis, where her husband is on the staff of Memphis State University, was formerly a teacher of English and Creative Writing at Abington High School near Philadelphia. Her poems have been widely published.

Wagner, Charles A., born in New York, raised in Lowell, Mass., a graduate of Columbia University, he was book and art critic of the late *New York Mirror,* and editor-in-chief of its Sunday Magazine, winning a Nieman Fellowship at Harvard in 1944. Executive Secretary of the PSA since 1963, his books are: *Poems of the Soil and the Sea,* (Knopf) ; *Nearer the Bone* (Coward-McCann) ; and for Boni an Anthology, *Prize Poems;* also a Harvard History titled: *Harvard: Four Centuries and Freedoms,* under a Dutton imprint. He won the First Prize of the PSA award for 1971 with his poem, "On Opening A Walnut."

Warren, Hamilton, born 1889, is a long-time member of the Society, whose poems have been widely published and heard over many radio stations. He has twice won the PSA annual First Prize, (1964, 1965) and has been one of only three to take both 1st and 2nd Annual Awards in the same year. A Connecticut resident, he is noted for his lyrics celebrating nature.

Warren, James E., Jr., A.B. and M.A.T. at Emory University, has published seven books and poetry pamphlets, and one book on the teaching of English. A Fellow of the International Institute of Arts and Letters, he was recognized in 1967 by the Georgia Writers Association, who accorded him their Literary Achievement Award, and in 1968 by the Writers' Club of Atlanta, who named him Writer of the Year.

WASSALL, IRMA, of Wichita, Kansas, has three volumes of verse, *Loonshadow* now in its second printing, *Drawings and Poems,* by Fred and Irma Wassall, and *Along the River,* a collection of haiku, published by Canada's *Haiku* in 1968. She has had some 900 poems published, in addition to short stories and articles. She is a dancer and singing guitarist as well, and organizer of the Wichita Society of the Classic Guitar.

WHEELOCK, JOHN HALL, has drawn poems from ten previous volumes for his latest, *By Daylight and in Dream, New and Collected Poems 1904–1970,* just published by Scribner's. Born in Far Rockaway, N.Y., graduate and post-graduate of Harvard, Göttingen, and Berlin Universities, his first was a joint collection with Van Wyck Brooke, *Verses by Two Undergraduates,* while still at Harvard. In addition to his poetry books, he has compiled and edited two prose works: *The Face of a Nation* and *Poetical Passages from the Writings of Thomas Wolfe.* An earlier volume of selected poems, *Poems Old and New,* 1956, won the Ridgely Torrence Memorial Award and the Borestone Mountain Poetry Award. Mr. Wheelock served for many years as an officer of Scribner's, and is a former vice president of the PSA.

WHITMAN, RUTH, whose second volume of poems, *The Marriage Wig,* was a co-winner, in MS, of the di Castagnola Award, and the year following its publication by Harcourt Brace (1968), won the Kovner Award of the Jewish Book Council of America, is a scholar-in-poetry at Radcliffe Institute and lives in Cambridge, Mass. with her painter husband. Two new books are scheduled for early publication: a collection of translations of the *Selected Poems of Jacob Glatstein,* with Introductory Essay and *The Passion of Lizzie Borden: New and Selected Poems.*

WIDDEMER, MARGARET, a Pennsylvanian long a New Yorker, began a prize-winning career in childhood, sharing a PSA-Pulitzer award with Carl Sandburg in 1919, and a *Saturday Review of Literature* award in 1923. A popular and prolific novelist, her poetry volumes include *Factories, Ballads and Lyrics, Hill Garden,* and *The Dark Cavalier, Collected Poems* published by

Doubleday. She edited the PSA *Jessie Rittenhouse Memoir-Anthology.*

WINCHELL, WALLACE, a native of New Jersey, where he was educated, has lived in the Midwest and in England. Co-winner of the 1970 di Castagnola Award, he has been published in this country and abroad.

WOLFE, ANN F., a free-lance writer of New York, formerly of Rochester, she has been a student at the College of St. Elizabeth in N.J., Columbia University, the Sorbonne, and the University of Marburg. She was at one time columnist for the *Paris Herald,* and has contributed to *The Saturday Review, The New York Times Book Review,* and others. A founder of the Poetry Workshop at Manhattan College, she is currently Book Review Editor of "The Recorder," Bulletin of the American Irish Historical Society.

WOLFERT, ADRIENNE, an assistant editor of *Poet Lore,* and contributor to *The New York Times* and others, she has written poetry and fiction since childhood. Two novels are in process. She is a volunteer in the School Volunteer Association, and is a special teacher of disadvantaged and disturbed boys, in addition to being involved in creative dramatics.

WORLEY, STELLA, born in Sacramento, Calif., received her education in New York City and was graduated from City College. She published her first poem at age ten, and has been writing ever since. Her most recent publications were in *Trace* and in *Poet Lore.* She has recently completed a book of poems concerning the distorting impact of social and cultural mores on the lives of individuals. She is married to a poet.

YOUNG, OLIVIA, whose poems appear in major periodicals and win many prizes, and whose book, *Take the Dirt Road,* came off the press in 1960, has two more volumes scheduled. She has been an instructor in poetry technique at Carmel and Santa Cruz, Educational Division, Calif., for the past ten years, and is currently director of workshops.

ZOLA, MARION, born in Brooklyn in 1945, and educated in public schools, attended Boston University, and studied with

John Malcolm Brinnin. Following graduation, she worked for Ford's Theatre Society and Harper and Row. Recently she taught English at Brandeis High School in New York City, and is at present a full-time student of Columbia Teachers' College.

Zucker, Jack, B.A. and M.A. of City College and N.Y.U., is now teaching at Philips Academy, Andover, Mass. His poems have appeared widely, and he has been offered fellowships by a number of well-known writers' conferences, as well as by the MacDowell Colony.

# *Acknowledgments*

Grateful acknowledgment is made to the following periodicals and book publishers for permission to reprint many of the poems herein:

*The Prairie Schooner,* the *Saturday Evening Post,* the *Oxford University Press,* the *Cambridge Review,* the *Chicago Tribune,* the *Literary Review,* the *New Yorker,* the *New York Herald-Tribune, Yankee, Writer's Digest,* the *Harvester,* the *Dietz Press* (Richmond, Va.), *Western Humanities Review, Roving Eye Press* (N.Y.), the *Lyric, New Mexico Quarterly Review,* the *Wings Press, Spirit, Harper's Magazine,* the *Virginia Quarterly Review,* the *Georgia Review, DeKalb Literary Arts Journal,* the *New York Times,* the *Quarterly Review of Literature, Steppenwolf,* the *Saturday Review, Bantam's, The World's Love Poetry, Harper & Brothers, David McKay Co., Simon & Schuster,* the *Colorado Quarterly, American Weave, Poetry* (Chicago), *Cyclotron, Aphra, Courier-Journal* (Louisville, Ky.), the *Christian Science Monitor, Fiddlehead, Variegation: A Free Verse Quarterly, Etc., A Review of General Semantics,* the *South Florida Poetry Journal, Simbolica,* the *Sign, Massachusetts Review, Yearbook of the Poetry Society of Georgia, Golden Goose* (Columbus, Ohio), *Atlantic Monthly, Voices, Poet Lore, Imprints Quarterly, Shenandoah, Manifold* (England), the *Ninth Hour, The Myth in the Vein* (Wake-Brook House), *Poetry Review,* the *Mathematics Teacher, Dryad, Trace, Kenyon Review,* the *University Review, Kansas Magazine, Hound and Unicorn* (Walton Press, Philadelphia), *Time of Singing, A Book of the Year, 1968* (The Poetry Society of Texas), the *Newsletter* (*American Symphony Orchestra League*), the *United Church Herald, Traveling Through the Dark* (Harper and Row), the *Southern Review, Bluebonnets and Blood* (Naylor Company, San Antonio), *Signature,* the *Human Voice, Blood and Milk Poems* (October House), *Selected Poems by Conrad Aiken* (Oxford University Press, special permission by Conrad Aiken), and to Charles Scribner's Sons for "Not We Alone" from *By Daylight and In Dream: New and Collected Poems, 1904–1970, by* John Hall Wheelock.